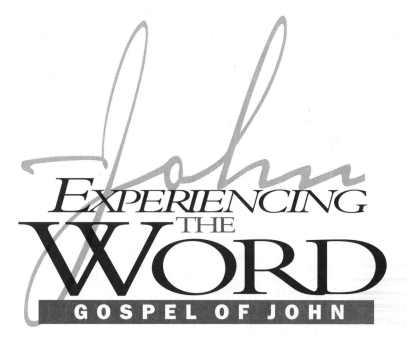

EXPERIENCING THE WORD

GOSPEL OF JOHN

WITH NOTES BY

HENRY BLACKABY

BEST-SELLING AUTHOR OF **EXPERIENCING GOD**

HOLMAN
CHRISTIAN
STANDARD
BIBLE™

The Gospel of John
The Holman Christian Standard Bible™
Copyright © 1999 by Broadman & Holman Publishers
All rights reserved

ISBN: 1-5581-9900-4

Printed in the United States
1 2 3 4 02 01 00 99
Q

The Holman Christian Standard Bible

B ible study is the road God's people take to hear and obey our Creator and Savior. The Holman Christian Standard Bible™ offers believers in the third millennium an up-to-date translation designed specifically for the needs of students of Scripture. It seeks to provide a translation as close to the words of the Hebrew and Greek texts as possible while still maintaining the literary quality and ease of reading that invite and enable people to read, study, and obey God's Word. To reach God's people effectively, a translation must provide a reverent, exalted text that is also reader friendly.

Translating the Bible into English offers a double challenge. First, each language has its own vocabulary, grammar, and syntax that cannot be exactly rendered into another language. Second, contemporary culture so honors relativism and individual freedom that it distrusts claims to absolute authority.

The first challenge means that English translators must avoid creating a special form of the language that does not communicate well to modern readers. For example John 1:6 in the original Greek reads, "was a man having been sent from God, name to him John." The English translator must provide a word order and syntax that follow the dynamics of the English language and that are familiar to English readers. In this instance, the Holman Christian Standard Bible™ reads, "There was a man named John who was sent from God." This accurately represents the original Greek text but also presents it in a form readers should find inviting and natural.

The second challenge means translators must hold firm to traditional beliefs about the authority of Scripture and avoid modern temptations to rewrite the Bible to say what modern readers want to hear. Translators must remember that the divine Author of the Bible inspired His Word for people today and for all time just as much as for the original audience. Translators who bow to modern relativism and change the text because of this perspective do so to their own spiritual detriment. The Holman Christian Standard Bible™ stands on the authority of God and has attempted to provide an accurate and readable translation of the Greek text of John's Gospel. The mission of the Holman Christian Standard Bible™ is to produce as precise a translation of the Hebrew, Aramaic, and Greek Scriptures as possible with the use of newly-published lexicons, grammars, and computer programs. The goal of this kind of translation is to encourage in-depth Bible study, but this translation also seeks to be highly readable (for public and private use) and also useful for personal memorization.

With these goals in view, an international and interdenominational team of more than seventy scholars has been formed to translate the Scriptures from the original languages. This translation project is being undertaken by Holman Bible Publishers, the oldest Bible publisher in America. Its origin can be traced back to a Philadelphia firm founded by Christopher Sower in 1743. Holman is spiritually grounded in the belief that the Bible is inerrant and is the sole authority for faith and practice in the life of a Christian.

In order to produce this translation, Holman Bible Publishers entered into a partnership with Dr. Art Farstad, former General Editor of the New King James Version. Art had been working on a new translation of the Bible for several years when in the Spring of 1998 he agreed to contract with Holman to complete the project. Art served as General Editor of this translation project until his death on September 1, 1998. His Assistant Editor and coworker, Dr. Ed Blum, former professor at Dallas Theological Seminary, picked up the mantle of leadership that Art left behind and now serves as General Editor of the Holman Christian Standard Bible™.

This edition of the Gospel of John contains several helpful features of the Holman Christian Standard Bible™. Notes immediately beneath the text of the translation refer to some of the variants in Greek manuscripts. Notes at the bottom of the page provide in significant places a literal rendering of the Greek text, other possible translations, explanations of biblical customs, places, and activities, and cross references to other passages. Word studies in the margins explain the precise meaning and application of prominent Greek words that appear in John's Gospel. The pronunciation of the Greek word for each Word Study is given in brackets. (See the Code for Pronunciation on page 62.)

As a further aid to understanding and incorporating the Bible into the reader's life, Dr. Henry Blackaby has provided spiritual insights that explain and apply truths from the Gospel of John that are related to knowing and doing God's will through "Experiencing the Word."

Seven Steps to Experiencing the Word

Do your morning devotions ever seem disconnected from the rest of your day? Do familiar Scriptures feel at home in the context of a worship service, but sound like wishful thinking in other arenas of life?

There's no doubt about it. You can *read* the words without *experiencing* the Word. But it doesn't have to be that way.

In the Gospel of John alone are numerous examples of this very idea—that you discover God's will by discovering who God is, that understanding Him requires a personal, ongoing relationship with His Word, that experiencing this Word brings you to a firsthand knowledge of the truth, and that owning this prized possession of eternal truth can set you free to become the person God wants you to be.

Not just reading the Word, but experiencing the Word is the only way.

Few people have been able to communicate this concept with such power, clarity, and commitment in recent years as Henry Blackaby, author of the *Experiencing God* book and study course. His methods for seeking God's will, listening for God's voice, and obeying God's teachings have helped millions truly begin experiencing God on a daily basis.

Again, John's Gospel captures the essence of this Christian desire in a nutshell—that your very life is profoundly dependent on a worshipful relationship with the God of the universe. The purpose of aligning yourself in harmony with God's will is to become a person God can use to touch others with His love. Both relationships—the vertical and the horizontal—are perfected through letting God's Word have its way in your life.

So every time you turn the page in this special edition of the Gospel of John, Henry Blackaby will meet you with another simple application of the Scripture—a fresh way to approach the Word, a practical tip for daily Christian living.

And by using the "Seven Steps to Experiencing the Word" index found on page vi of this book, you can walk verse-by-verse through this proven outline, and watch the Word begin to take shape in your life.

SEVEN STEPS TO
Experiencing the Word
IN THE GOSPEL OF JOHN

5. Know God's Will by Knowing God's Heart

You never have to sense an emptiness or lack of purpose. He will always fill your life with Himself. When you have Him, you have everything there is.

6. Obey. Obey. And Keep on Obeying.

Adjust your life to God in the kind of relationship where you follow Him wherever He leads you—even if the assignment seems to be small or insignificant.

7. Let Witnessing Spill Out of Worship

When the world sees things happening through God's people that cannot be explained except that God Himself has done them, then the world will be drawn to the God they see.

GREEK WORD STUDIES

JOHN

PROLOGUE

1 In the beginning was the Word,[a]
and the Word was with God,
and the Word was God.
[2] He was with God in the beginning.
[3] All things were created through Him,
and apart from Him not one thing was created
that has been created.
[4] In Him was life,
and that life was the light of men.
[5] That light shines in the darkness,
yet the darkness did not overcome[b] it.
[6] There was a man named John
who was sent from God.
[7] He came as a witness
to testify about the light,
so that all might believe through him.[c]
[8] He was not the light,
but he came to testify about the light.
[9] The true light, who gives light to everyone,
was coming into the world.[d]
[10] He was in the world,
and the world was created through Him,
yet the world did not know Him.
[11] He came to His own,
and His own people[e] did not receive Him.

---

[a] 1:1 *The Word* (Gk *Logos*) is a title for Jesus as the communication and revealer of God the Father (see 1:14; Rev 19:13).

[b] 1:5 Or *grasp, comprehend, overtake* (see 12:35)

[c] 1:7 Or *it* (the light)

[d] 1:9 Or *The true light who comes into the world gives light to everyone.*

[e] 1:11 The same Gk adjective is used twice in this verse: the first refers to all that Jesus owned as Creator (*to His own*); the second refers to the Jews (*His own people*).

WORD STUDY

Greek word: **logos** [LAH gahss]
Translation: **Word, word**
Uses in John's Gospel: **40**
Uses in John's writings: **65**
Uses in the NT: **330**
Key passages: **John 1:1,14**

Like the related verb *lego (to speak),* the noun *logos* most often refers to either oral or written communication. It means *statement* or *report* in some contexts, but most often in John's Gospel (and in the NT in general) *logos* refers to God's Word (i.e. the Old Testament) or to Jesus' words. Thus, the primary use of *logos* is to denote divine revelation in some form or another. John used the term in its most exalted sense when he personified *logos* to refer to Christ. The *Logos* eternally existed as God (the Son) and with God (the Father)—He was in fact the Creator (Jn 1:3)—but He became a human being (v. 14), Jesus of Nazareth, so that He could reveal the Father and His will for humanity (v. 18).

¹²But to all who did receive Him,
He gave them the right to be[a] children of God,
to those who believe in His name,
¹³who were born,
not of blood,[b]
or of the will of the flesh,
or of the will of man,[c]
but of God.
¹⁴The Word became flesh[d]
and took up residence[e] among us.
We observed His glory,
the glory as the only[f] Son[g] from the Father,
full of grace and truth.
¹⁵(John testified concerning Him and exclaimed,
"This was the One of whom I said,
'The One coming after me has surpassed me,
because He existed before me.'")
¹⁶For we have all received grace after grace
from His fullness.
¹⁷For the law was given through Moses;
grace and truth came through Jesus Christ.
¹⁸No one has ever seen God.[h]
The only[i] Son[1]—
the One who is at the Father's side[j]—
He has revealed Him.

[1]**1:18** Other mss read *God.* This reading would allow the translation to be *the only God,* which presents theological problems in light of the doctrine of the Trinity, or *the only One, Himself God,* but this requires an explanation of Gk grammar not found elsewhere.

[a]**1:12** Or *become*
[b]**1:13** Lit *bloods.* The plural form of *blood* occurs only here in the New Testament. It may refer either to lineal descent (i.e. blood from one's father and mother) or to the Old Testament sacrificial system (i.e. the various blood sacrifices). Neither is the basis for birth into the family of God.
[c]**1:13** Or *not of human lineage, or of human capacity, or of human volition.*
[d]**1:14** The eternally existent Word (vv. 1–2) took on full humanity, but without sin (Heb 4:15).
[e]**1:14** Lit *and tabernacled* or *and dwelt in a tent:* this word occurs only here in John. A related word, referring to the Feast of Tabernacles, occurs only in 7:2.
[f]**1:14** Or *only begotten* or *incomparable;* the Gk word could refer to someone's only child (Lk 7:12; 8:42; 9:38) or someone's special child (Heb 11:17).
[g]**1:14** *Son* is implied from the reference to the Father and from Gk usage (see previous note).
[h]**1:18** Since God is an infinite being, no one can see Him in His absolute essential nature (see Ex 33:18–23).
[i]**1:18** See note at v. 14.
[j]**1:18** Lit *is in the bosom of the Father*

JOHN THE BAPTIST'S TESTIMONY

¹⁹ This is John's testimony when the Jews^a from Jerusalem sent priests and Levites to ask him, "Who are you?"

²⁰ He confessed and did not deny, declaring,^b "I am not the Messiah."^c

²¹ "What then?" they asked him. "Are you Elijah?"

"I am not," he said.

"Are you the Prophet?"

"No," he answered.

²² "Who are you, then?" they asked. "We need to give an answer to those who sent us. What can you tell us about yourself?"

²³ He said, "I am **'A voice of one crying out: In the wilderness make straight the way of the Lord'**^d— just as Isaiah the prophet said."

²⁴ Now they had been sent from the Pharisees. ²⁵ So they asked him, "Why then do you baptize if you aren't the Messiah,^e or Elijah, or the Prophet?"

²⁶ "I baptize in^f water," John answered them. "But among you stands Someone you don't know. ²⁷ He is the One coming after me,[1] whose sandal strap I'm not worthy to untie."

²⁸ All this happened in Bethany across the Jordan,^g where John was baptizing.

THE LAMB OF GOD

²⁹ The next day John^h saw Jesus coming toward him and said, "Here is the Lamb of God, who takes away the sin of the world! ³⁰ This is the One I told you about: 'After me comes a man who has surpassed me, because He existed before me.' ³¹ I didn't know Him, but I came baptizing inⁱ water so He might be revealed to Israel."

³² And John testified, "I watched the Spirit descending from heaven like a dove, and He rested upon Him.

The Way to God's Will Is Through God's Son

Knowing God does not come through a program, a study, or a method. Knowing God comes through a relationship with a Person.

But to all who did receive Him, He gave them the right to be children of God, to those who believe in His name.

—John 1:12

He Must Increase, We Must Decrease

The call to salvation is a call to be on mission with Him. In this new relationship you move into a servant role with God as your Lord and Master.

"This is the One I told you about: 'After me comes a man who has surpassed me, because He existed before me.'"

—John 1:30

---

[1] **1:27** Some manuscripts add *who came before me*

---

^a**1:19** In John *the Jews* usually indicates the Jewish authorities who led the nation.
^b**1:20** Lit *he confessed*
^c**1:20** See note at v. 41
^d**1:23** Isa 40:3
^e**1:25** See note at v. 41

^f**1:26** Or *with*
^g**1:28** Another Bethany was near Jerusalem (the home of Lazarus, Martha, and Mary; see 11:1).
^h**1:29** Lit *he*
ⁱ**1:31** Or *with*

[33] I didn't know Him, but He[a] who sent me to baptize in[b] water told me, 'The One on whom you see the Spirit descending and resting—He is the One baptizing in[b] the Holy Spirit.' [34] I have seen and testified that He is the Son of God!"[1]

[35] Again the next day, John was standing with two of his disciples. [36] When he saw Jesus passing by, he said, "Look! The Lamb of God!"

[37] The two disciples heard him say this and followed Jesus. [38] When Jesus turned and noticed them following Him, He asked them, "What are you looking for?"

They said to Him, "Rabbi" (which means "Teacher"[c]), "where are you staying?"

[39] "Come and you'll see," He replied. So they went and saw where He was staying, and they stayed with Him that day. It was about ten in the morning.[d]

[40] Andrew, Simon Peter's brother, was one of the two who heard John and followed Him. [41] He first found his own brother Simon and told him, "We have found the Messiah!" (which means "Anointed One"[e]) [42] and brought him to Jesus.

When Jesus saw him, He said, "You are Simon, son of John.[2] You will be called Cephas"[f] (which means "Rock").

PHILIP AND NATHANAEL

[43] The next day He[g] decided to leave for Galilee. Jesus found Philip and told him, "Follow Me!"

[44] Now Philip was from Bethsaida, the hometown of Andrew and Peter. [45] Philip found Nathanael[h] and told

By Knowing God, You Can Help Others Know Him

People know us. They know what we can do. When they see things happen that can only be explained by God's involvement, they will come to know Him.

He first found his own brother Simon and told him, "We have found the Messiah!" (which means "Anointed One") and brought him to Jesus.

—John 1:41–42a

[1]1:34 A few mss read *is the Chosen One of God*
[2]1:42 Other mss read *Simon, son of Jonah*

[a]1:33 *He* refers to God the Father, who gave John a sign to help him identify the Messiah. Vv. 32–34 indicate that John did not know that Jesus was the Messiah until the Spirit descended upon Him at His baptism.
[b]1:33 Or *with*
[c]1:38 *Rabbi* means *my great one* in Hb but was used of a recognized teacher of the Scriptures (1:49; 3:2; 4:31; 6:25; 9:2; 11:8); see the Aramaic *Rabbouni* in 20:9.
[d]1:39 Lit *about the tenth hour;* or *four in the afternoon.* Various methods of reckoning time were used in the ancient world. John probably used a different method than the other three Gospels.
[e]1:41 In the New Testament the word *Messiah* translates the Gk word *Christos* ("Anointed One") except here and in 4:25, where it translates *Messias.*
[f]1:42 *Cephas* is Aramaic for *rock* (Gk *petros,* the same word used for Peter's name, as in v. 40).
[g]1:43 Or *he,* referring either to Peter (see v. 42) or Andrew (see vv. 40–41)
[h]1:45 Probably the Bartholomew of the other Gospels and Acts

him, "We have found the One of whom Moses wrote in the law (and so did the Prophets): Jesus the son of Joseph, from Nazareth!"

⁴⁶ "Can anything good come out of Nazareth?" Nathanael asked him.

"Come and see," Philip answered.

⁴⁷ Then Jesus saw Nathanael coming toward Him and said about him, "Here is a true Israelite in whom is no deceit."

⁴⁸ "How do you know me?" Nathanael asked.

"Before Philip called you, when you were under the fig tree, I saw you," Jesus answered.

⁴⁹ "Rabbi," Nathanael replied, "You are the Son of God! You are the King of Israel!"

⁵⁰ Jesus responded to him, "Do you believe only[a] because I told you I saw you under the fig tree? You will see[b] greater things than this." ⁵¹ Then He said, "I assure you:[c] You will see[d] heaven opened and the angels of God ascending and descending upon the Son of Man."[e]

THE FIRST SIGN: TURNING WATER INTO WINE

2 On the third day a wedding took place in Cana of Galilee. Jesus' mother was there, and ² Jesus and His disciples were invited to the wedding as well. ³ When the wine ran out, Jesus' mother told Him, "They don't have any wine."

⁴ "What has this concern of yours to do with Me,[f] woman?"[g] Jesus asked. "My hour[h] has not yet come."

⁵ "Do whatever He tells you," His mother told the servants.

WORD STUDY

Greek word: **amen** [ah MAYN]
Translation: **assure**
Uses in John's Gospel: **50**
Uses in John's writings: **59**
Uses in the NT: **129**
Key passage: **John 1:51**

The English word *amen* comes from a Hebrew verb meaning *to trust, believe,* which is related to the noun for *truth, faith,* or *faithfulness.* It is common for Christians to end a prayer with the word *amen;* this occurs often in the Bible also. But Jesus used *amen* as part of a formula to introduce certain statements that He considered especially important (literally, *amen, I say to you*). This occurs thirty-one times in Matthew, thirteen times in Mark, and six times in Luke. The emphasis in Jesus' use of this term was on the certainty of what He was about to say. In John's Gospel all twenty-five sayings have the double *amen* (literally, *amen, amen, I say to you*), which seems to add a tone of seriousness to His statement. Jesus normally used these special formulae to introduce truths about God, Jesus, the Spirit, or some aspect of salvation.

ᵃ**1:50** *only* added for clarity
ᵇ**1:50** *You* is singular in Gk and refers to Nathanael.
ᶜ**1:51** *I assure you* is lit *amen, amen I say to you.* The double form of *amen* is used only in John (25 times). The term *amen* transliterates a Hb word expressing affirmation (Dt 27:15; 1 Kgs 1:36; Jer 28:6; Ps 106:48). Jesus used it to testify to the certainty and importance of His words (see Rev 3:14).
ᵈ**1:51** *You* is plural in Gk and refers to Nathanael and the other disciples.
ᵉ**1:51** The phrase *Son of Man* was

Jesus' most common way to refer to Himself and comes from Dan 7:13–14.
ᶠ**2:4** Or *You and I see things differently;* lit *What to Me and to you?* (see Mt 8:29; Mk 1:24; 5:7; Lk 8:28; Jdg 11:12; 2 Sam 16:10; 19:22; 1 Kgs 17:18; 2 Kgs 3:13; 2 Chr 35:21)
ᵍ**2:4** The word *woman* was not a term of disrespect in Gk (see 4:21; 8:10; 20:13,15), but was a striking way for Jesus to address His mother (see 19:26).
ʰ**2:4** I.e. the time of his sacrificial death and exaltation (see 7:30; 8:20; 12:23,27; 13:1; 17:1)

WORD STUDY

Greek word: **semeion**
[say MIGH ahn]
Translation: **sign**
Uses in John's Gospel: **16**
Uses in John's writings: **23**
Uses in the NT: **77**
Key passages: **John 2:11; 4:54; 20:30**

The three main terms that describe miracles in the NT are *semeion (sign), dunamis (power),* and *teras (wonder).* One problem in studying these three words is that some English versions use the term "miracle" to translate all three words, at least in some contexts. The word *teras* is the least common of the three (sixteen times) and always refers to miracles; *dunamis* and *semeion* occur numerous times and refer to other phenomena besides miracles. The word *teras* is always accompanied by *semeion* and sometimes by *dunamis* also (Acts 2:22; 2 Cor. 12:12; 2 Thes. 2:9; Heb. 2:4). The distinction between the three terms is one of emphasis: *semeion* refers to the purpose of the miracle; *dunamis* refers to the source that enables someone to perform a miracle; and *teras* refers to the reaction of the crowd when a miracle was performed. John's favorite term for Jesus' miracles was *semeion (dunamis* does not occur and *teras* occurs only once, 4:48), for he emphasized the purpose for these miracles: they revealed who Jesus was so that people would believe in Him (20:30–31). In contrast to the other Gospels, John provides only seven *signs* in his Gospel (the first two are numbered, 2:11; 4:54), but he reminds us that Jesus performed many others (20:30).

⁶ Now six stone water jars had been set there for Jewish purification. Each contained twenty or thirty gallons.ᵃ

⁷ "Fill the jars with water," Jesus told them. So they filled them to the brim. ⁸ Then He said to them, "Now draw some out and take it to the chief servant."ᵇ And they did.

⁹ When the chief servant tasted the water (after it had become wine), he did not know where it came from—though the servants who had drawn the water knew. He called the groom ¹⁰ and told him, "Everybody sets out the fine wine first, then, after people have drunk freely, the inferior. But you have kept the fine wine until now."

¹¹ Jesus performed this first signᶜ in Cana of Galilee. He displayed His glory, and His disciples believed in Him.

¹² After this He went down to Capernaum, together with His mother, His brothers, and His disciples, and they stayed there only a few days.

CLEANING OUT THE TEMPLE COMPLEX

¹³ The Jewish Passover was near, so Jesus went up to Jerusalem. ¹⁴ In the temple complexᵈ He found people selling oxen, sheep, and doves, and He also foundᵉ the money changers sitting there. ¹⁵ After making a whip out of cords, He drove everyone out of the temple complex with their sheep and oxen. He also poured out the money changers' coins and overturned the tables. ¹⁶ He told those who were selling doves, "Get these things out of here! Stop turning my Father's house into a marketplace!"ᶠ

¹⁷ And His disciples remembered that it is written: **"Zeal for Your house will consume Me."**ᵍ

¹⁸ So the Jews replied to Him, "What sign of authorityʰ will You show us for doing these things?"

ᵃ2:6 Lit *two or three measures*
ᵇ2:8–9 Lit *ruler of the table;* perhaps *master of the feast* or *head-waiter*
ᶜ2:11 Lit *this beginning of the signs* (see 4:54; 20:30). There are seven miraculous signs in John's Gospel and are so noted in the headings.
ᵈ2:14 The temple complex included the sanctuary (the Holy Place and the Holy of Holies), at least four courtyards (for priests, Jews, women, and Gentiles), numerous gates, and several covered walkways.
ᵉ2:14 *He also found* added for clarity
ᶠ2:16 Lit *a house of business*
ᵍ2:17 Ps 69:9
ʰ2:18 *of authority* added for clarity

¹⁹ Jesus answered, "Destroy this sanctuary,ᵃ and I will raise it up in three days."

²⁰ Therefore the Jews said, "This sanctuary took forty-six years to build, and will You raise it up in three days?"

²¹ But He was speaking about the sanctuary of His body. ²² So when He was raised from the dead, His disciples remembered that He had said this. And they believed the Scripture and the statement Jesus had made.

²³ While He was in Jerusalem at the Passover festival, many trusted in His name when they saw the signs He was doing. ²⁴ Jesus, however, would not entrust Himself to them, since He knew them all ²⁵ and because He did not need anyone to testify about man; for He Himself knew what was in man.

JESUS AND NICODEMUS

3 There was a man from the Pharisees named Nicodemus, a ruler of the Jews. ² This man came to Him at night and said, "Rabbi, we know that You have come from God as a teacher, for no one could perform these signs You do unless God were with him."

³ Jesus replied, "I assure you:ᵇ Unless someone is born again,ᶜ he cannot see the kingdom of God."

⁴ "But how can anyone be born when he is old?" Nicodemus asked Him. "Can he enter his mother's womb a second time and be born?"

⁵ Jesus answered: "I assure you:ᵈ Unless someone is born of water and the Spirit,ᵉ he cannot enter the kingdom of God. ⁶ Whatever is born of the flesh is flesh, and whatever is born of the Spirit is spirit. ⁷ Do not be amazed that I told you that youᶠ must be born again. ⁸ The windᵍ blows where it pleases, and you hear its sound, but you don't know where it comes from or where it is going. So it is with everyone born of the Spirit."

⁹ "How can these things be?" asked Nicodemus.

¹⁰ "Are you a teacherʰ of Israel and don't know these things?" Jesus replied. ¹¹ "I assure you:ⁱ We speak what

---

ᵃ2:19 See note at 2:14
ᵇ3:3 See note at 1:51
ᶜ3:3 The same Gk word can mean *again* or *from above* (also in v. 7).
ᵈ3:5 See note at 1:51
ᵉ3:5 Or *spirit, wind* (see note at v. 8)
ᶠ3:7 The pronoun is plural in Gk.
ᵍ3:8 The Gk word *pneuma* can mean *wind, spirit,* or *Spirit,* each of which occurs in this context.
ʰ3:10 Or *the teacher*
ⁱ3:11 See note at 1:51

WORD STUDY

Greek word: **anothen**
[AH noh thuhn]
Translation: **again**
Uses in John's Gospel: **5**
Uses in John's writings: **5**
Uses in the NT: **13**
Key passages: **John 3:3,7**

The expression *born again* comes from John 3:3, where Jesus tells Nicodemus that he must be born (*gennao,* the term used for the genealogy in Mt 1:1–17) again *(anothen).* The term *anothen* can mean *again* or *from above,* but the meaning *again* for *anothen* occurs only in Galatians 4:9 in the NT. All other uses of the term mean *from above* (see Jn 3:31; 19:11,23; Jms 1:17; 3:15,17) or something similar (such as *top* in Mt 27:51; Mk 15:38). It is likely that Nicodemus misunderstood Jesus' use of *anothen,* thinking He meant *again* as in a second time. This is why Nicodemus responded the way he did, by a reference to physical birth (v. 4). But Jesus went on to indicate that He was referring to the other meaning of *anothen,* a birth *from above,* a birth from the Spirit (Jn 3:5,6,8).

WORD STUDIES

Greek word: *monogenes*
[mah nah gehn AYSS]

Translation: **only**

Uses in John's Gospel: **4**

Uses in John's writings: **5**

Uses in the NT: **9**

Key passages: **John 1:14,18;
3:16,18; 1 John 4:9; Heb 11:17**

English translations have traditionally understood *monogenes* to be from *monos (only)* and *gennao (beget),* thus following the Latin Vulgate *(unigenitus).* This has caused great misunderstanding since God the Son did not have an origin and was not in any sense begotten or created by God. He is Himself an eternal being. Therefore, it is best to understand *monogenes* to be from *monos (only)* and *genos (kind,* Latin *genus),* meaning *the only one of its kind.* This is much more consistent with John's five uses of the word, and support for this translation is found in Hebrews 11:17 where Isaac is called Abraham's *monogenes.* Isaac was not Abraham's only-begotten son (Ishmael was his firstborn and there were other sons through Keturah), but Isaac was the only one of his kind—the son of promise. Luke's three uses of the word (7:12; 8:42; 9:38) may refer to a special child, not just an only child, though this is not clear. In the Old Latin translation, *monogenes* was translated as *unicus,* from which we get our word *unique.* This is what is meant by *monogenes* in John's writings (Jn 1:14,18; 3:16,18; 1 Jn 4:9): Jesus is God's only Son in that His essential nature is the same as the Father's. There are many children of God (see Jn 1:12–13), but there is only one Son of God.

We know and We testify to what We have seen, but you[a] do not accept Our testimony.[b] 12 If I have told you about things that happen on earth and you don't believe, how will you believe if I tell you about things of heaven? 13 No one has ascended into heaven except the One who descended from heaven—the Son of Man.[1] 14 Just as Moses lifted up the serpent in the wilderness, so the Son of Man must be lifted up, 15 so that everyone who believes in Him will[2] have eternal life.

16 "For God loved the world in this way: He gave His only[c] Son, so that everyone who believes in Him will not perish but have eternal life. 17 For God did not send His Son into the world that He might judge the world, but that the world might be saved through Him. 18 Anyone who believes in Him is not judged, but anyone who does not believe is already judged, because he has not believed in the name of the only[d] Son of God.

19 "This, then, is the judgment: the light has come into the world, and people loved darkness rather than the light, because their deeds were evil. 20 For everyone who practices wicked things hates the light and avoids it,[e] so that his deeds may not be exposed. 21 But anyone who lives by[f] the truth comes to the light, so that his works may be shown to be accomplished by God."[g]

JESUS AND JOHN THE BAPTIST

22 After this Jesus and His disciples went to the Judean countryside, where He spent time with them and baptized. 23 John also was baptizing in Aenon near Salim, because there was plenty of water there. And people were coming and being baptized, 24 since John had not yet been thrown into prison.

25 Then a dispute arose between John's disciples and a Jew[h] about purification. 26 So they came to John and told him, "Rabbi, the One you testified about, and who was

[1] 3:13 Other mss add *who is in heaven*
[2] 3:15 Other mss add *not perish, but*

---

[a] 3:11 The word *you* in Gk is plural here and in v. 12.
[b] 3:11 The plurals (*We, Our*) refer to Jesus and His authority to speak for the Father.
[c] 3:16 Or *only begotten* (see note at 1:14)
[d] 3:18 See note at 1:14.

[e] 3:20 Lit *and does not come to the light*
[f] 3:21 Lit *who does*
[g] 3:21 It is possible that Jesus' words end at v. 15. (Ancient Gk did not have quotation marks.)
[h] 3:25 See note at 1:19.

with you across the Jordan, is baptizing—and everyone is flocking to Him."

²⁷ John responded, "No one can receive a single thing unless it's given to him from heaven. ²⁸ You yourselves can testify that I said, 'I am not the Messiah,ᵃ but I've been sent ahead of Him.' ²⁹ He who has the bride is the groom. But the groom's friend, who stands by and listens for him, rejoices greatlyᵇ at the groom's voice. So this joy of mine is complete. ³⁰ He must increase, but I must decrease."

THE ONE FROM HEAVEN

³¹ The One who comes from above is above all. The one who is from the earth is earthly and speaks in earthly terms.ᶜ The One who comes from heaven is above all. ³² He testifies to what He has seen and heard, yet no one accepts His testimony. ³³ The one who has accepted His testimony has affirmed that God is true. ³⁴ For He whom God sent speaks God's words, since He gives the Spirit without measure. ³⁵ The Father loves the Son and has given all things into His hands. ³⁶ The one who believes in the Son has eternal life, but the one who refuses to believe in the Son will not see life; instead, the wrath of God remains on him.

JESUS AND
THE SAMARITAN WOMAN

4 When Jesus¹ knew that the Pharisees heard He was making and baptizing more disciples than John ² (though Jesus Himself was not baptizing, but His disciples were), ³ He left Judea and went again to Galilee. ⁴ He had to travel through Samaria, ⁵ so He came to a town of Samaria called Sychar near the propertyᵈ that Jacob had given his son Joseph. ⁶ Jacob's well was there, and Jesus, worn out from His journey, sat down at the well. It was about six in the evening.ᵉ

⁷ A woman of Samaria came to draw water.

"Give Me a drink," Jesus said to her, ⁸ for His disciples had gone into town to buy food.

---

¹4:1 Other mss read *the Lord*

ᵃ3:28 Or *the Christ*
ᵇ3:29 Lit *with joy rejoices*
ᶜ3:31 Or *of earthly things*

ᵈ4:5 Lit *piece of land*
ᵉ4:6 Lit *the sixth hour;* see note at 1:39

Give God Room to Prove Himself to You

We come to know God as we experience Him. We can know about God as a Provider, but we really come to know God as Provider when we experience Him providing something for our lives.

"I assure you: We speak what We know and We testify to what We have seen."

—John 3:11a

Jesus Offers Everything That a Person Really Needs

The cross, the death of Jesus Christ, and His resurrection are God's final, total, and complete expression that He loves us.

"For God loved the world in this way: He gave His only Son, so that everyone who believes in Him will not perish but have eternal life. For God did not send His Son into the world that He might judge the world, but that the world might be saved through Him."

—John 3:16–17

WORD STUDY

Greek word: **zoe** [zoh AY]
Translation: **life**
Uses in John's Gospel: **36**
Uses in John's writings: **66**
Uses in the NT: **135**
Key passages: **John 3:15–16; 4:14; 17:2–3**

What is the meaning of life? The most important aspect of life is a relationship with God. The essence of life is union; the essence of death is separation. Physical life is the union of body and spirit; physical death is the separation of the body and spirit. Spiritual life is union or oneness with God through faith in Christ; spiritual death is separation from God. Life—spiritual life—means more than mere existence. It refers to a relationship with God. This is the life that Jesus came to give us, and He intended us to enjoy the blessings of that life, that relationship, "abundantly" (Jn 10:10).

Therefore, everyone will exist forever, but not everyone will *live* forever. Unbelievers will experience death forever, "the second death" (Rev 20:14), eternal separation from God in the lake of fire. But by God's grace Christians have "eternal redemption" (Heb 9:12) or "eternal life" (Jn 3:15–16; 4:14). The phrase "eternal life" occurs 43 times in the NT—23 of them in John and 1 John—and refers to the permanence of the relationship believers have with God even now. Eternal life is knowing the Father and the Son (Jn 17:2–3). This is God's never-ending gift to those who trust in Christ (Rom 6:23). Truly, this is the meaning of *life*.

[9] "How is it that You, a Jew, ask for a drink from me, a Samaritan woman?" she asked.[a] For Jews do not associate with[b] Samaritans.[1]

[10] Jesus answered, "If you knew the gift of God, and who is saying to you, 'Give Me a drink,' you would ask Him, and He would give you living water."

[11] "Sir," said the woman, "You don't even have a bucket, and the well is deep. So where do you get this 'living water'? [12] You aren't greater than our father Jacob, are you? He gave us the well and drank from it himself, as did his sons and livestock."

[13] Jesus said, "Everyone who drinks from this water will get thirsty again. [14] But whoever drinks from the water that I will give him will never get thirsty again—ever! In fact, the water I will give him will become a well[c] of water springing up within him for eternal life."

[15] "Sir," the woman said to Him, "give me this water so I won't get thirsty and come here to draw water."

[16] "Go call your husband," He told her, "and come back here."

[17] "I don't have a husband," she[d] answered.

"You have correctly said, 'I don't have a husband,'" Jesus said. [18] "For you've had five husbands, and the man you now have is not your husband. What you have said is true."

[19] "Sir," the woman replied, "I see that You are a prophet. [20] Our fathers worshiped on this mountain,[e] yet you Jews[f] say that the place to worship is in Jerusalem."

[21] Jesus told her, "Believe Me, woman,[g] an hour is coming when you will worship the Father neither on this mountain nor in Jerusalem. [22] You Samaritans[h] worship what you do not know. We worship what we do know, because salvation is from the Jews. [23] But an hour is coming, and is now here, when the true worshipers will worship the Father in spirit and truth. Yes, the Father wants such people to worship Him. [24] God is

---

[1] 4:9 Other mss omit *For Jews do not associate with Samaritans.*

---

[a] 4:9 Lit *the Samaritan woman asked Him*
[b] 4:9 Or *do not share vessels with*
[c] 4:14 Or *spring*
[d] 4:17 Lit *the woman*
[e] 4:20 I.e., Mount Gerizim, where

there had been a Samaritan temple that rivaled Jerusalem's.
[f] 4:20,22 *Jews* implied
[g] 4:21 See note at 2:4
[h] 4:22 *Samaritans* is implied since the Gk verb is plural.

Spirit, and those who worship Him must worship in spirit and truth."

²⁵ The woman said to Him, "I know that Messiah is coming" (who is called Christ[a]). "When He comes, He will explain everything to us."

²⁶ "I am He,"[b] Jesus told her, "the One speaking to you."

THE RIPENED HARVEST

²⁷ Just then His disciples arrived, and they were amazed that He was talking with a woman. Yet no one said, "What do You want?" or "Why are You talking with her?"

²⁸ Then the woman left her water jar, went into town, and told the men, ²⁹ "Come, see a man who told me everything I ever did! Could this be the Messiah?" ³⁰ They left the town and made their way to Him.

³¹ In the meantime the disciples kept urging Him, "Rabbi, eat something."

³² But He said, "I have food to eat that you don't know about."

³³ The disciples said to one another, "Could someone have brought Him something to eat?"

³⁴ "My food is to do the will of Him who sent Me and to finish His work," Jesus told them. ³⁵ "Don't you say, 'There are still four more months, then comes the harvest'? Listen to what I'm telling you:[c] Open[d] your eyes and look at the fields, for they are ready[e] for harvest. ³⁶ The reaper is already receiving pay and gathering fruit for eternal life, so the sower and reaper can rejoice together. ³⁷ For in this case the saying is true: 'One sows and another reaps.' ³⁸ I sent you to reap what you didn't labor for; others have labored, and you have benefited from[f] their labor."

THE SAVIOR OF THE WORLD

³⁹ Now many Samaritans from that town believed in Him because of what the woman said[g] when she testified, "He told me everything I ever did." ⁴⁰ Therefore, when the Samaritans came to Him, they asked Him to

Learn to Think the Way God Thinks

The adjusting is always to a Person. You adjust your life to God. You adjust your viewpoints to be like His viewpoints. You adjust your ways to be like His ways.

"God is Spirit, and those who worship Him must worship in spirit and truth."

—John 4:24

His Plan Takes Precedence Over Yours

God is far more interested in accomplishing His kingdom purposes than you are. He will move you into every assignment that He knows you are ready for.

"My food is to do the will of Him who sent Me and to finish His work," Jesus told them.

—John 4:34

---

[a]4:25 See note at 1:41
[b]4:26 Lit *I am*
[c]4:35 Lit *Look, I'm telling you*
[d]4:35 Lit *Raise*
[e]4:35 Lit *white*
[f]4:38 Lit *you have entered into*
[g]4:39 Lit *because the woman's word*

stay with them, and He stayed there two days. [41] Many more believed because of what He said.[a] [42] And they told the woman, "We no longer believe because of what you said, for we have heard for ourselves and know that this really is the Savior of the world."[1]

A GALILEAN WELCOME

[43] After two days He left there for Galilee. [44] Jesus Himself testified that a prophet has no honor in his own country. [45] When they entered Galilee, the Galileans welcomed Him because they had seen everything He did in Jerusalem during the festival. For they also had gone to the festival.

THE SECOND SIGN: HEALING AN OFFICIAL'S SON

[46] Then He went again to Cana of Galilee, where He had turned the water into wine. There was a certain royal official whose son was ill at Capernaum. [47] When this man heard that Jesus had come from Judea into Galilee, he went to Him and pleaded with Him to come down and heal his son, for he was about to die.

[48] Jesus told him, "Unless you people[b] see signs and wonders, you will not believe."

[49] "Sir," the official said to Him, "come down before my boy dies!"

[50] "Go," Jesus told him, "your son will live." The man believed what[c] Jesus said to him and departed.

[51] While he was still going down, his slaves met him saying that his boy was alive. [52] He asked them at what time he got better. "Yesterday at seven in the morning [d] the fever left him," they answered. [53] The father realized this was the very hour at which Jesus had told him, "Your son will live." Then he himself believed, along with his whole household.

[54] This therefore was the second sign[e] Jesus performed after He came from Judea to Galilee.

[1]4:42 Other mss add *the Messiah*

You Believe by Faith, Know by Experience

Knowledge of God comes through experience. We come to know God as we experience Him in and around our lives.

And they told the woman, "We no longer believe because of what you said, for we have heard for ourselves and know that this really is the Savior of the world."

—John 4:42

---

[a]4:41 Lit *because of His word*
[b]4:48 *people* implied
[c]4:50 Lit *the word*

[d]4:52 Lit *the seventh hour;* or *at one in the afternoon;* see 1:39 note
[e]4:54 2:11

THE THIRD SIGN:
HEALING THE SICK

5 After this a Jewish festival took place, and Jesus went up to Jerusalem. [2] By the Sheep Gate in Jerusalem there is a pool, called Bethesda[1] in Hebrew,[a] which has five colonnades.[b] [3] Within these lay a multitude of the sick—blind, lame, and paralyzed—⌐waiting for the moving of the water, [4] because an angel would go down into the pool from time to time and stir up the water. Then the first one who got in after the water was stirred up recovered from whatever ailment he had.⌐[2]

[5] One man was there who had been sick for thirty-eight years. [6] When Jesus saw him lying there and knew he had already been there a long time, He said to him, "Do you want to get well?"

[7] "Sir," the sick man answered, "I don't have a man to put me into the pool when the water is stirred up, but while I'm coming, someone goes down ahead of me."

[8] "Get up," Jesus told him, "pick up your bedroll and walk!" [9] Instantly the man got well, picked up his bedroll, and started to walk.

Now that day was the Sabbath, [10] so the Jews said to the man who had been healed, "This is the Sabbath! It's illegal for you to pick up your bedroll."

[11] He replied, "The man who made me well told me, 'Pick up your bedroll and walk.'"

[12] "Who is this man who told you, 'Pick up your bedroll[c] and walk?'" they asked. [13] But the man who was cured did not know who it was, because Jesus had slipped away into the crowd that was there.[d]

[14] After this Jesus found him in the temple complex and said to him, "See, you are well. Do not sin any more, so that something worse doesn't happen to you." [15] The man went and reported to the Jews that it was Jesus who had made him well.

Trust and Obey

When you are convinced of His love, you can believe Him and trust Him. When you trust Him, you can obey Him.

He replied, "The man who made me well told me, 'Pick up your bedroll and walk.'"

—John 5:11

[1]5:2 Other mss read *Bethzatha*
[2]5:3-4 Other mss omit the words in brackets

[a]5:2 I.e. Aramaic
[b]5:2 I.e. rows of columns supporting a roof
[c]5:12 *your bedroll* added for clarity
[d]5:13 Lit *slipped away, there being a crowd in that place*

HONORING THE FATHER
AND THE SON

[16] Therefore, the Jews began persecuting Jesus[1] because He was doing these things on the Sabbath. [17] But Jesus responded to them, "My Father is still working, and I also am working." [18] This is why the Jews began trying all the more to kill Him: not only was He breaking the Sabbath, but He was even calling God His own Father, making Himself equal with God.

[19] Then Jesus replied, "I assure you:[a] The Son is not able to do anything on His own, but only what He sees the Father doing. For whatever the Father[b] does, these things the Son also does in the same way. [20] For the Father loves the Son and shows Him everything He is doing, and He will show Him greater works than these so that you will be amazed. [21] And just as the Father raises the dead and gives them life, so also the Son gives life to whomever He wishes. [22] The Father, in fact, judges no one but has given all judgment to the Son, [23] so that all people will honor the Son just as they honor the Father. Anyone who does not honor the Son does not honor the Father who sent Him.

LIFE AND JUDGMENT

[24] "I assure you:[c] Anyone who hears My word and believes Him who sent Me has eternal life and will not come under judgment, but has passed from death to life.

[25] "I assure you:[c] An hour is coming, and is now here, when the dead will hear the voice of the Son of God, and those who hear will live. [26] For just as the Father has life in Himself, so also He has granted to the Son to have life in Himself. [27] And He has granted Him the right to pass judgment, because He is the Son of Man. [28] Do not be amazed at this, because a time is coming when all who are in the graves will hear His voice [29] and come out—those who have done good things, to the resurrection of life, but those who have done wicked things, to the resurrection of judgment.

[1]**5:16** Other mss add *and trying to kill Him*

[a]**5:19** See note at 1:51
[b]**5:19** Lit *whatever that One*
[c]**5:24, 25** See note at 1:51

Make Sure You're Asking the Right Questions

"What is God's will for my life?" is not the best question to ask. I think the right question is simply, "What is God's will?" The focus needs to be on God and His purposes, not my life.

"I can do nothing on My own. Only as I hear do I judge, and My judgment is righteous, because I do not seek My own will, but the will of Him who sent Me."

—John 5:30

Stay in the Word and Know What God Says

When you come to understand the spiritual meaning and application of a Scripture passage, God's Spirit has been at work. This does not *lead* you to an encounter with God. That *is* the encounter with God. When God speaks to you through the Bible, He is relating to you in a personal and real way.

"You pore over the Scriptures because you think you have eternal life in them, yet they testify about Me."

—John 5:39

³⁰ "I can do nothing on My own. Only as I hear do I judge, and My judgment is righteous, because I do not seek My own will, but the will of Him who sent Me.

FOUR WITNESSES TO JESUS

³¹ "If I testify about Myself, My testimony is not valid.ᵃ ³² There is Another who testifies about Me, and I know that the testimony He gives about Me is valid.ᵃ ³³ You peopleᵇ have sent messengersᶜ to John, and he has testified to the truth. ³⁴ I don't receive man's testimony, but I say these things so that you may be saved. ³⁵ Johnᵈ was a burning and shining lamp, and for an hour you were willing to enjoy his light.

³⁶ "But I have a greater testimony than John's because of the works that the Father has given Me to accomplish. These very works I am doing testify about Me that the Father has sent Me. ³⁷ The Father who sent Me has Himself testified about Me. You have not heard His voice at any time, and you haven't seen His form. ³⁸ You don't have His word living in you, because you don't believe the One He sent. ³⁹ You pore overᵉ the Scriptures because you think you have eternal life in them, yet they testify about Me. ⁴⁰ And you are not willing to come to Me that you may have life.

⁴¹ "I do not accept glory from men, ⁴² but I know you—that you have no love for God within you. ⁴³ I have come in My Father's name, yet you don't accept Me. If someone else comes in his own name, you will accept him. ⁴⁴ How can you believe? While accepting glory from one another, you don't seek the glory that comes from the only God. ⁴⁵ Do not think that I will accuse you to the Father. Your accuser is Moses, on whom you have set your hope. ⁴⁶ For if you believed Moses, you would believe Me, because he wrote about Me. ⁴⁷ But if you don't believe his writings, how will you believe My words?"

THE FOURTH SIGN:
FEEDING FIVE THOUSAND

6 After this Jesus crossed the Sea of Galilee (or Tiberias). ² And a huge crowd was following Him because they saw the signs that He was performing on the sick.

ᵃ5:31–32 Or *true*
ᵇ5:33 *people* added for clarity
ᶜ5:33 *messengers* supplied for clarity
ᵈ5:35 Lit *that man*
ᵉ5:39 In Gk this could be a command ("Pore over").

WORD STUDY

Greek word: ***martureo***
[mahr tyew REH oh]
Translation: **testify, witness**
Uses in John's Gospel: **33**
Uses in John's writings: **47**
Uses in the NT: **76**
Key passage: **John 5:31–39**

The Greek verb *martureo* was a legal term in the ancient world, just as *testify* is today in English. The same is true of other related Greek words, such as *marturia* and *marturion* (both meaning *testimony* or *witness* with an emphasis on that which is stated), and *martus* (*witness,* the person testifying); the English word *martyr* is derived from *martus.* The legal concept was not always in view for these words in Greek usage, and in fact the court setting is rarely involved in the NT. The general ideas implied by testifying and witnessing are always there, however, such as persons declaring certain things to be factual and providing evidence to validate their claims. John 5 is not a legal setting, but Jesus used *martureo* seven times and *marturia* four times to provide four evidences that validate His claims about Himself and His relationship to the Father (vv. 17–30): John the Baptist (vv. 31–35); the works Christ performed (v. 36); the Father (vv. 37–38); and the Scriptures (vv. 39–47).

³ So Jesus went up a mountain and sat down there with His disciples.

⁴ Now the Passover, a Jewish festival, was near. ⁵ Therefore, when Jesus raised His eyes and noticed a huge crowd coming toward Him, He asked Philip, "Where will we buy bread so these people can eat?" ⁶ He asked this to test him, for He Himself knew what He was going to do.

⁷ Philip answered, "Two hundred denarii[a] worth of bread wouldn't be enough for each of them to have a little."

⁸ One of His disciples, Andrew, Simon Peter's brother, said to Him, ⁹ "There's a boy here who has five barley loaves and two fish—but what are they for so many?"

¹⁰ Then Jesus said, "Have the people sit down."

There was plenty of grass in that place, so the men sat down, numbering about five thousand.[b] ¹¹ Then Jesus took the loaves, and after giving thanks He distributed them to those who were seated; so also with the fish, as much as they wanted.

¹² When they were full, He told His disciples, "Collect the leftovers so that nothing is wasted." ¹³ So they collected them and filled twelve baskets with the pieces from the five barley loaves that were left over by those who had eaten.

¹⁴ When the people saw the sign[1] He had done, they said, "This really is the Prophet who was to come into the world!" ¹⁵ Therefore, when Jesus knew that they were about to come and take Him by force to make Him king, He withdrew again[2] to the mountain by Himself.

THE FIFTH SIGN: WALKING ON WATER

¹⁶ When evening came, His disciples went down to the sea, ¹⁷ got into a boat, and started across the sea to Capernaum. Darkness had already set in, but Jesus had not yet come to them. ¹⁸ Then a high wind arose, and the sea began to churn. ¹⁹ After they had rowed about

Take Faithfulness Over Success

The outward appearance of success does not always indicate faith, and the outward appearance of failure does not always indicate that faith is lacking. A faithful servant is one that does what his Master tells him whatever the outcome may be.

"Don't work for the food that perishes but for the food that lasts for eternal life, which the Son of Man will give you, because on Him God the Father has set His seal of approval."

—John 6:27

¹6:14 Other mss read *signs*
²6:15 Other mss omit *again;* a previous withdrawal is mentioned in Mark 6:31–32, an event that occurred just before the feeding of the five thousand.

[a]6:7 A denarius was a Roman silver coin worth about a day's wage for a common laborer.

[b]6:10 Or *they sat down, the men numbering about five thousand*

three or four miles,[a] they saw Jesus walking on the sea. He was coming near the boat, and they were afraid. [20] But He said to them, "It is I.[b] Don't be afraid!" [21] Then they were willing to take Him on board, and at once the boat was at the shore where they were heading.

THE BREAD OF LIFE

[22] The next day, the crowd that had stayed on the other side of the sea knew there had been only one boat. They also knew[c] that Jesus had not boarded the boat with His disciples, but His disciples had gone off alone. [23] Some boats from Tiberias came near the place where they ate the bread after the Lord gave thanks. [24] When the crowd saw that neither Jesus nor His disciples were there, they got into the boats and went to Capernaum, looking for Jesus.

[25] When they found Him on the other side of the sea, they said to Him, "Rabbi, when did You get here?"

[26] Jesus answered, "I assure you:[d] You are looking for Me, not because you saw the signs, but because you ate the loaves and were filled. [27] Don't work for the food that perishes but for the food that lasts for eternal life, which the Son of Man will give you, because on Him God the Father has set His seal of approval."

[28] "What can we do to perform the works of God?" they asked.

[29] Jesus replied, "This is the work of God: that you believe in the One He has sent."

[30] "Then what sign are You going to do so we may see and believe You?" they asked. "What are You going to perform? [31] Our fathers ate the manna in the desert, just as it is written: **'He gave them bread from heaven to eat.'**[e]

[32] Jesus said to them, "I assure you:[f] Moses didn't give you the bread from heaven, but My Father gives you the true bread from heaven. [33] For the bread of God is the One who comes down from heaven and gives life to the world."

[34] Then they said, "Sir, give us this bread always!"

[35] "I am the bread of life," Jesus told them. "No one

---

a**6:19** Lit *twenty-five or thirty stadia*
b**6:20** Lit *I am*
c**6:22** *They also knew* added for clarity
d**6:26** See note at 1:51
e**6:31** Ps 78:24; Ex 16:4, 15
f**6:32** See note at 1:51

WORD STUDY

Greek word: ***pisteuo***
[pihss TYEW oh]
Translation: **believe**
Uses in John's Gospel: **98**
Uses in John's writings: **107**
Uses in the NT: **241**
Key passages: **John 3:16; 6:29–47; 20:31**

The Greek word *pisteuo* means *to believe, trust, rely upon,* and its related noun is *pistis (faith).* In his Gospel, John never used the words *repent, repentance,* or *faith* to describe the way people are saved. Instead, he used *believe* since this term included all these ideas. John preferred the verb form to emphasize the act that is necessary for someone to be saved—total dependence on the work of Another. John did indicate, however, that believing can be superficial; that is, it can be merely intellectual without resulting in true salvation (Jn 2:23–24; 12:42–43; see Jms 2:19). But John's main thrust is that complete reliance upon Jesus the Messiah and Son of God (20:31) for salvation gives eternal life to the person who believes (3:16; 6:47). Jesus used a word play when He said that people must do "the work of God" for salvation, for His point was that we must not try to work for it at all. We must simply "believe in the One He has sent" (6:29).

who comes to Me will ever be hungry, and no one who believes in Me will ever be thirsty again. [36] But as I told you, you've seen Me, and yet you do not believe. [37] Everyone the Father gives Me will come to Me, and the one who comes to Me I will never cast out. [38] For I have come down from heaven, not to do My will, but the will of Him who sent Me. [39] This is the will of Him who sent Me: that I should lose none of those He has given Me but should raise them up on the last day. [40] For this is the will of My Father: that everyone who sees the Son and believes in Him may have eternal life, and I will raise him up on the last day."

[41] Therefore the Jews started complaining about Him, because He said, "I am the bread that came down from heaven." [42] They were saying, "Isn't this Jesus the son of Joseph, whose father and mother we know? How can He now say, 'I have come down from heaven'?"

[43] Jesus answered them, "Stop complaining among yourselves. [44] No one can come to Me unless the Father who sent Me draws[a] him, and I will raise him up on the last day. [45] It is written in the Prophets: **'And they will all be taught by God.'**[b] Everyone who has listened to and learned from the Father comes to Me— [46] not that anyone has seen the Father except the One who is from God. He has seen the Father.

[47] "I assure you:[c] Anyone who believes[1] has eternal life. [48] I am the bread of life. [49] Your fathers ate the manna[d] in the desert, and they died. [50] This is the bread that comes down from heaven so that anyone may eat of it and not die. [51] I am the living bread that came down from heaven. If anyone eats of this bread he will live forever. The bread that I will give for the life of the world is My flesh."

[52] At that, the Jews argued among themselves, "How can this man give us His flesh to eat?"

[53] So Jesus said to them, "I assure you:[e] Unless you eat the flesh of the Son of Man and drink His blood, you do not have life in yourselves. [54] Anyone who eats My flesh

Live in a Constant State of Availability

If you want to meet a need through my life, I am your servant; and I will do whatever is required.

_____

"For I have come down from heaven, not to do My will, but the will of Him who sent Me."

—John 6:38

---

[1]**6:47** Other mss add *in Me*

---

[a]**6:44** Or *brings, leads;* see the use of this Gk verb in 12:32; 21:6; Acts 14:19; Jms 2:6.
[b]**6:45** Isa 54:13
[c]**6:47** See note at 1:51

[d]**6:49** Bread miraculously provided by God for the Israelites (see Ex 16:12–36)
[e]**6:53** See note at 1:51

and drinks My blood has eternal life, and I will raise him up on the last day, [55] because My flesh is true food and My blood is true drink. [56] The one who eats My flesh and drinks My blood lives in Me, and I in him. [57] Just as the living Father sent Me and I live because of the Father, so the one who feeds on Me will live because of Me. [58] This is the bread that came down from heaven; it is not like the bread[a] your fathers ate—and they died. The one who eats this bread will live forever."

[59] He said these things while teaching in the synagogue in Capernaum.

MANY DISCIPLES DESERT JESUS

[60] Therefore, when many of His disciples heard this, they said, "This teaching is hard! Who can accept[b] it?"

[61] Jesus, knowing in Himself that His disciples were complaining about this, asked them, "Does this offend you? [62] Then what if you were to observe the Son of Man ascending to where He was before? [63] The Spirit is the One who gives life. The flesh doesn't help at all. The words that I have spoken to you are spirit and are life. [64] But there are some among you who don't believe." (For Jesus knew from the beginning those who would not believe and the one who would betray Him.) [65] He said, "This is why I told you that no one can come to Me unless it is granted to him by the Father."

[66] From that moment many of His disciples turned back and no longer walked with Him. [67] Therefore Jesus said to the Twelve, "You don't want to go away too, do you?"

[68] Simon Peter answered, "Lord, to whom should we go? You have the words of eternal life. [69] And we have come to believe and know that You are the Holy One of God!"[1]

[70] Jesus replied to them, "Didn't I choose you, the Twelve? Yet one of you is the Devil!"[c] [71] He was referring to Judas, Simon Iscariot's son,[2] one of the Twelve, because he was going to betray Him.

[1]**6:69** Other mss read *You are the Messiah, the Son of the Living God*
[2]**6:71** Lit *Judas, of Simon Iscariot;* some mss read *Judas Iscariot, Simon's son*

[a]**6:58** *the bread* added for clarity   [c]**6:70** Or *a devil;* see 13:2, 27
[b]**6:60** Lit *hear*

Depend on God for Everything

Do you realize that the Lord does not just give you life—He is your life?

"Just as the living Father sent Me and I live because of the Father, so the one who feeds on Me will live because of Me."
—John 6:57

You Run on God's Power, Not Manpower

You do not get orders, then go out and carry them out on your own. You relate to God, respond to Him, and adjust your life so that He can do what He wants through you.

"The Spirit is the One who gives life. The flesh doesn't help at all. The words that I have spoken to you are spirit and are life."
—John 6:63

THE UNBELIEF
OF JESUS' BROTHERS

7 After this Jesus traveled in Galilee, since He did not want to travel in Judea because the Jews[a] were trying to kill Him. [2] The Jewish festival of Tabernacles[b] was near, [3] so His brothers said to Him, "Leave here and go to Judea so Your disciples can see Your works that You are doing. [4] For no one does anything in secret while he's seeking public recognition. If You do these things, show Yourself to the world." [5] (For not even His brothers believed in Him.)

[6] Jesus told them, "My time has not yet arrived, but your time is always at hand. [7] The world cannot hate you, but it does hate Me because I testify about it—that its deeds are evil. [8] Go up to the festival yourselves. I'm not going up to the festival yet,[1] because My time has not yet fully come." [9] After He had said these things, He stayed in Galilee.

JESUS AT THE FESTIVAL
OF TABERNACLES

[10] When His brothers had gone up to the festival, then He also went up, not openly but secretly. [11] The Jews[c] were looking for Him at the festival and saying, "Where is He?" [12] And there was a lot of discussion about Him among the crowds. Some were saying, "He's a good man." Others were saying, "No, on the contrary, He's deceiving the people." [13] Still, nobody was talking publicly about Him because they feared the Jews.[c]

[14] When the festival was already half over, Jesus went up into the temple complex and began to teach. [15] Then the Jews[c] were amazed and said, "How does He know the Scriptures, since He hasn't been trained?"

[16] Jesus answered them, "My teaching isn't Mine, but is from the One who sent Me. [17] If anyone wants to do His will, he will understand whether the teaching is from God or if I am speaking on My own. [18] The one who speaks for himself seeks his own glory. But He who seeks the glory of the One who sent Him is true, and

His Calling Will Be
Bigger Than You Are

The kind of assignments God gives in the Bible are always God-sized. They are always beyond what people can do because He wants to demonstrate His nature, His strength, His provision, and His kindness to His people and to a watching world. That is the only way the world will come to know Him.

Then the Jews were amazed and said, "How does He know the Scriptures, since He hasn't been trained?" Jesus answered them, "My teaching isn't Mine, but is from the One who sent Me."

—John 7:15–16

---

[1] 7:8 Other mss omit *yet*

---

[a] 7:1 See note at 1:19
[b] 7:2 One of three great Jewish religious festivals, along with Passover and Pentecost (see Ex 23:14; Dt 16:16)
[c] 7:11, 13, 15 See note at 1:19

unrighteousness is not in Him. ¹⁹ Didn't Moses give you the law? Yet none of you keeps the law! Why do you want to kill Me?"

²⁰ "You have a demon!" the crowd responded. "Who wants to kill You?"

²¹ "I did one work, and you are all amazed," Jesus answered. ²² "Consider this:ᵃ Moses has given you circumcision—not that it comes from Moses but from the fathers—and you circumcise a man on the Sabbath. ²³ If a man receives circumcision on the Sabbath so that the law of Moses won't be broken, are you angry at Me because I made a man entirely well on the Sabbath? ²⁴ Stop judging according to outward appearances; rather judge according to righteous judgment."

THE IDENTITY OF THE MESSIAH

²⁵ Some of the people of Jerusalem were saying, "Isn't this the man they want to kill? ²⁶ Yet, look! He's speaking publicly and they're saying nothing to Him. Can it be true that the authorities know He is the Messiah?ᵇ ²⁷ But we know where this man is from. When the Messiah comes, nobody will know where He is from."

²⁸ As He was teaching in the temple complex, Jesus cried out, "You know Me and you know where I am from. Yet I have not come on My own, but the One who sent Me is true. You don't know Him; ²⁹ I know Him because I am from Him, and He sent Me."

³⁰ Therefore they tried to seize Him. Yet no one laid a hand on Him because His hourᶜ had not yet come. ³¹ However, many from the crowd believed in Him and said, "When the Messiah comes, He won't perform more signs than this man has done, will He?"

³² The Pharisees heard the crowd muttering these things about Him, so the chief priests and the Phariseesᵈ sent temple police to arrest Him.

³³ Therefore Jesus said, "I am only with you for a short time. Then I'm going to the One who sent Me. ³⁴ You will look for Me, and you will not find Me; and where I am, you cannot come."

³⁵ Then the Jewsᵉ said to one another, "Where does

Let Others See Jesus in You

Let the world see God at work and He will attract people to Himself. Let Christ be lifted up—not in words, but in life.

"If anyone wants to do His will, he will understand whether the teaching is from God or if I am speaking on My own."

—John 7:17

ᵃ**7:22** Lit *Because of this*
ᵇ**7:26** Or *the Christ*
ᶜ**7:30** See note at 2:4
ᵈ**7:32** *the chief priests and the Phar-* isees refers to the Sanhedrin, the highest Jewish court
ᵉ**7:35** See note at 1:19

WORD STUDY

Greek word: **hudor** [HOO dohr]

Translation: **water**

Uses in John's Gospel: **21**

Uses in John's writings: **43**

Uses in the NT: **76**

Key passages: **John 3:5; 7:38**

The English prefix *hydr-* (as in *hydrolic*) comes from the Greek word for water, *hudor*. This word often refers to literal water, of course, but *water* often has a symbolic or supernatural connotation in the Bible. This is particularly true in John's Gospel: Jesus changed water into wine as His first sign (2:1–11); Jesus offered "living water" to the woman at the well, which referred to Himself as the giver and sustainer of eternal life (4:7–26); the water in the pool of Bethesda had healing powers (5:2–7); Jesus washed the disciples feet to symbolize our relationship to Him and mutual servanthood (13:1–16); and when the soldier pierced Jesus' side after His death, "blood and water" came forth, symbolizing death ("blood," Jesus really died) and life ("water," Jesus will rise from the dead; see 1 Jn 5:6–8). Twice water is used as a symbol of the Holy Spirit: the Spirit effects the new birth ("born of water and Spirit"; see 3:5–8), and the Spirit is the living water that Jesus promised to those who believe in Him (7:37–39; see Rev 22:1,17).

He intend to go so we won't find Him? He doesn't intend to go to the Dispersion[a] among the Greeks and teach the Greeks, does He? [36] What is this remark He made: 'You will look for Me and you will not find Me; and where I am, you cannot come'?"

THE PROMISE OF THE SPIRIT

[37] On the last and most important day of the festival, Jesus stood up and cried out, "If anyone is thirsty, he should come to Me and drink! [38] The one who believes in Me, as the Scripture has said,[b] will have streams of living water flow from deep within him." [39] He said this about the Spirit, whom those who believed in Him were going to receive, for the Spirit[1] had not yet been received,[c][2] because Jesus had not yet been glorified.

THE PEOPLE ARE DIVIDED OVER JESUS

[40] When some from the crowd heard these words, they said, "This really is the Prophet!" [41] Others said, "This is the Messiah!" But some said, "Surely the Messiah doesn't come from Galilee, does He? [42] Doesn't the Scripture say that the Messiah comes from David's offspring[d] and from the town of Bethlehem, where David once lived?" [43] So a division occurred among the crowd because of Him. [44] Some of them wanted to seize Him, but no one laid hands on Him.

DEBATE OVER JESUS' CLAIMS

[45] Then the temple police came to the chief priests and Pharisees,[e] who asked them, "Why haven't you brought Him?"

[46] The police answered, "No man ever spoke like this!"

[1]**7:39** Other mss read *Holy Spirit*
[2]**7:39** Other mss read *had not yet been given*

[a]**7:35** I.e. Jewish people scattered among Gentile lands. They spoke Gk and were influenced by Gk culture.
[b]**7:38** Jesus may have had several Old Testament passages in mind, and the main possibilities are Isa 58:11; Jer 2:13; 17:13; Ezk 47:1–12; Zch 14:8; see also Jn 4:10,11; Rev 7:17; 22:1.
[c]**7:39** Lit *the Spirit was not yet;* the word *received* is implied from the previous sentence.
[d]**7:42** Lit *seed*
[e]**7:45** See note at v. 32

⁴⁷ Then the Pharisees responded to them: "Are you fooled too? ⁴⁸ Have any of the rulers believed in Him? Or any of the Pharisees? ⁴⁹ But this crowd, which doesn't know the law, is accursed!"

⁵⁰ Nicodemus—the one who came to Him previously, being one of them—said to them, ⁵¹ "Our law doesn't judge a man before it hears from him and knows what he's doing, does it?"

⁵² "You aren't from Galilee too, are you?" they replied. "Search and see: no prophet arises from Galilee."ᵃ

¹⌐⁵³ So each one went to his house.

8 But Jesus went to the Mount of Olives.

AN ADULTERESS FORGIVEN

² At dawn He went to the temple complex again, and all the people were coming to Him. He sat down and began to teach them.

³ Then the scribes and the Pharisees brought a woman caught in adultery, making her stand in the center. ⁴ "Teacher," they said to Him, "this woman was caught in the act of committing adultery. ⁵ In the law Moses commanded us to stone such women. So what do You say?" ⁶ They asked this to trap Him, in order that they might have evidence to accuse Him.

Jesus stooped down and started writing on the ground with His finger. ⁷ When they persisted in questioning Him, He stood up and said to them, "The one without sin among you should be the first to throw a stone at her."

⁸ Then He stooped down again and continued writing on the ground. ⁹ When they heard this, they left one by one, starting with the older men. Only He was left, with the woman in the center. ¹⁰ When Jesus stood up, He said to her, "Woman,ᵇ where are they? Has no one condemned you?"

¹¹ "No one, Lord,"ᶜ she answered.

"Neither do I condemn you," said Jesus. "Go, and from now on do not sin any more."⌐

---

¹**7:53** Other mss do not contain the verses in brackets (7:53—8:11).

ᵃ**7:52** Jonah (2 Kgs 14:25) and probably other prophets did come from Galilee.

ᵇ**8:10** See note at 2:4
ᶜ**8:11** Or *Sir*; see 4:15,49; 5:7; 6:34; 9:36

Your Relationship with Christ Colors Everything

Everything in your Christian life, everything about knowing Him and experiencing Him, everything about knowing His will depends on the quality of your love relationship to God.

"The one who believes in Me, as the Scripture has said, will have streams of living water flow from deep within him."

—John 7:38

Make the Sacrifices of Right Choices

Until you are ready to make any adjustment necessary to follow and obey what God has said, you will be of little use to God. Your greatest single difficulty in following God may come at the point of the adjustment.

When Jesus stood up, He said to her, "Woman, where are they? Has no one condemned you?"
"No one, Lord," she answered.
"Neither do I condemn you," said Jesus. "Go, and from now on do not sin any more."

—John 8:10–11

WORD STUDY

Greek word: **phos** [FOHSS]
Translation: **light**
Uses in John: **23**
Uses in John's writings: **33**
Uses in the NT: **73**
Key passages: **John 1:4–5;
8:12; 9:5**

The word *phos* is seldom used in the literal sense in the NT. Most often it is a metaphor referring to holiness, purity, or godliness. Jesus used the term in the Sermon on the Mount to describe His disciples and the holy standard of conduct that He expected them to model to the world (Mt 5:14–16; 6:23). In John's Gospel, however, Jesus Himself is "the light," as stated in the Prologue (1:4–5) and in Jesus' own words (8:12; 9:5). In this case, the light is revelatory and reflects God's character or holiness; in other words, *the light* refers to God's revelation or disclosure of Himself to the world in the incarnation (1:4–9). Incredibly, those in darkness prefer the darkness, at least until they accept the truth of God's revelation in His Son and believe in the light (3:19–21; 8:12; 12:46).

¹² Then Jesus spoke to them again: "I am the light of the world. Anyone who follows Me will never walk in the darkness, but will have the light of life."

JESUS' SELF-WITNESS

¹³ So the Pharisees said to Him, "You are testifying about Yourself. Your testimony is not valid."ᵃ

¹⁴ "Even if I testify about Myself," Jesus replied, "My testimony is valid,ᵇ because I know where I came from and where I'm going. But you don't know where I come from or where I'm going. ¹⁵ You judge by human standards.ᶜ I judge no one. ¹⁶ And if I do judge, My judgment is true, because I am not alone, but I and the Father who sent Me judge together.ᵈ ¹⁷ Even in your law it is written that the witness of two men is valid. ¹⁸ I am the One who testifies about Myself, and the Father who sent Me testifies about Me."

¹⁹ Then they asked Him, "Where is Your Father?"

"You know neither Me nor My Father," Jesus answered. "If you knew Me, you would also know My Father." ²⁰ He spoke these words by the treasury,ᵉ while teaching in the temple complex. But no one seized Him, because His hourᶠ had not come.

JESUS PREDICTS HIS DEPARTURE

²¹ Then He said to them again, "I'm going away; you will look for Me, and you will die in your sin. Where I'm going, you cannot come."

²² So the Jews said again, "He won't kill Himself, will He, since He says, 'Where I'm going, you cannot come'?"

²³ "You are from below," He told them, "I am from above. You are of this world; I am not of this world. ²⁴ Therefore I told you that you will die in your sins. For if you do not believe that I am He,ᵍ you will die in your sins."

²⁵ "Who are You?" they questioned.

ᵃ**8:13** The law of Moses required at least two witnesses to make a claim legally valid (v. 17).
ᵇ**8:14** Or *true*
ᶜ**8:15** Lit *You judge according to the flesh*
ᵈ**8:16** *judge together* added for clarity

ᵉ**8:20** A place for offerings to be given, perhaps in the court of women
ᶠ**8:20** See note at 2:4
ᵍ**8:24** Lit *I am;* Jesus claimed to be deity (see note at 6:20), but the Pharisees didn't understand His meaning.

"Precisely what I've been telling you from the very beginning," **Jesus told them.** [26] "I have many things to say and to judge about you, but the One who sent Me is true, and what I have heard from Him—these things I tell the world."

[27] They did not know He was speaking to them about the Father. [28] So Jesus said to them, "When you lift up the Son of Man, then you will know that I am He,[a] and that I do nothing on My own. But just as the Father taught Me, I say these things. [29] The One who sent Me is with Me. He has not left Me alone, because I always do what pleases Him."

TRUTH AND FREEDOM

[30] As He was saying these things, many believed in Him. [31] So Jesus said to the Jews who had believed Him, "If you continue in My word,[b] you really are My disciples. [32] You will know the truth, and the truth will set you free."

[33] "We are descendants[c] of Abraham," they answered Him, "and we have never been enslaved to anyone. How can You say, 'You will become free'?"

[34] Jesus responded, "I assure you:[d] Everyone who commits sin is a slave of sin. [35] A slave does not remain in the household forever, but a son does remain forever. [36] Therefore if the Son sets you free, you really will be free. [37] I know you are descendants[e] of Abraham, but you are trying to kill Me because My word[f] is not welcome among you. [38] I speak what I have seen in the presence of the Father, and therefore you do what you have heard from your father."

[39] "Our father is Abraham!" they replied.

"If you were Abraham's children," **Jesus told them,** "you would do what Abraham did. [40] But now you are trying to kill Me, a man who has told you the truth that I heard from God. Abraham did not do this! [41] You're doing what your father does."

"We weren't born of fornication," they said. "We have one Father—God."

[42] Jesus said to them, "If God were your Father, you would love Me, because I came from God and I am here.

You Are Never as Free as When You're Following God

When God gives you a command, He is trying to protect and preserve the best He has for you. He is not restricting you. He is freeing you.

So Jesus said to the Jews who had believed Him, "If you continue in My word, you really are My disciples. You will know the truth, and the truth will set you free."

—John 8:31-32

---

[a]**8:28** See note at 8:24
[b]**8:31** Or *My teaching;* or *My message*
[c]**8:33** Or *offspring;* lit *seed* (see 7:42)
[d]**8:34** See note at 1:51
[e]**8:37** See note at v. 33
[f]**8:37** See note at v. 31

For I didn't come on My own, but He sent Me. [43] Why don't you understand what I say? Because you cannot listen to[a] My word. [44] You are of your father the Devil, and you want to carry out your father's desires. He was a murderer from the beginning and has not stood in the truth, because there is no truth in him. When he tells a lie, he speaks from his own nature,[b] because he is a liar and the father of liars.[c] [45] Yet because I tell the truth, you do not believe Me. [46] Who among you can convict Me of sin? If I tell the truth, why don't you believe Me? [47] The one who is from God listens to God's words. This is why you don't listen, because you are not from God."

JESUS AND ABRAHAM

[48] The Jews responded to Him, "Aren't we right in saying that You're a Samaritan and have a demon?"

[49] "I do not have a demon," Jesus answered. "On the contrary, I honor My Father and you dishonor Me. [50] I do not seek My glory; the One who seeks it also judges. [51] I assure you:[d] If anyone keeps My word, he will never see death—ever!"

[52] Then the Jews said, "Now we know You have a demon. Abraham died and so did the prophets. You say, 'If anyone keeps My word, he will never taste death—ever!' [53] Are You greater than our father Abraham who died? Even the prophets died. Who do You pretend to be?"[e]

[54] "If I glorify Myself," Jesus answered, "My glory is nothing. My Father is the One who glorifies Me, of whom you say, 'He is our God.' [55] You've never known Him, but I know Him. If I were to say I don't know Him, I would be a liar like you. But I do know Him, and I keep His word. [56] Your father Abraham was overjoyed that he would see My day; he saw it and rejoiced."

[57] The Jews replied, "You aren't fifty years old yet, and You've seen Abraham?"[1]

[1]**8:57** Other mss read *and Abraham has seen You?*

God Is Speaking. Are You Listening?

Does God really speak to His people in our day? Yes! Will He reveal to you where He is working when He wants to use you? Yes! God has not changed. He still speaks to His people.

"The one who is from God listens to God's words."

—John 8:47a

[a]**8:43** Or *hear*
[b]**8:44** Lit *from his own things*
[c]**8:44** Lit *of it*
[d]**8:51** See note at 1:51
[e]**8:53** Lit *Who do You make Yourself?*

⁵⁸ Jesus said to them, "I assure you:ᵃ Before Abraham was, I am."ᵇ

⁵⁹ At that, they picked up stones to throw at Him. But Jesus was hiddenᶜ and went out of the temple complex.¹

THE SIXTH SIGN:
HEALING A MAN BORN BLIND

9 As He was passing by, He saw a man blind from birth. ² His disciples questioned Him: "Rabbi, who sinned, this man or his parents, that he was born blind?"

³ "Neither this man sinned nor his parents," Jesus answered. "This came aboutᵈ so that God's works might be displayed in him. ⁴ We² must do the works of Him who sent Me while it is day. Night is coming when no one can work. ⁵ As long as I am in the world, I am the light of the world."

⁶ After He said these things He spit on the ground, made some mud from the saliva, and spread the mud on his eyes. ⁷ "Go," He told him, "wash in the pool of Siloam" (which means "Sent"). So he left, washed, and came back seeing.

⁸ His neighbors and those who formerly had seen him as a beggar said, "Isn't this the man who sat begging?" ⁹ Some said, "He's the one." "No," others were saying, "but he looks like him."

He kept saying, "I'm the one!"

¹⁰ Therefore they asked him, "Then how were your eyes opened?"

¹¹ He answered, "The man called Jesus made mud, spread it on my eyes, and told me, 'Go to Siloam and wash.' So when I went and washed I received my sight."

¹² "Where is He?" they asked.

"I don't know," he said.

THE HEALED MAN'S TESTIMONY

¹³ They brought to the Pharisees the man who used to be blind. ¹⁴ The day that Jesus made the mud and

Take Your Orders One Day at a Time

God doesn't usually give you a one-time assignment and leave you there forever. Yes, you may be placed in one job at one place for a long time, but God's assignments come to you on a daily basis.

"We must do the works of Him who sent Me while it is day."

—John 9:4a

---

¹**8:59** Other mss add *and having gone through their midst, He passed by*
²**9:4** Other mss read *I*

ᵃ**8:58** See note at 1:51
ᵇ**8:58** *I AM* is the name God gave Himself at the burning bush (see Ex 3:13–14); see note at 4:26; 8:24.
ᶜ**8:59** Or *Jesus hid Himself*
ᵈ**9:3** *This came about* added for clarity

WORD STUDY

Greek word: **hamartolos**
[hah mahr toh LAHSS]

Translation: **sinner**

Uses in John: **4**

Uses in John's writings: **4**

Uses in the NT: **47**

Key passages: **John 9:16,24,25,31**

One of the key doctrines of the Christian faith is that all people are sinners and need Jesus as their Savior so they may have eternal life. This teaching is consistent with the use of the word *hamartolos (sinner)* in several places and with other related passages about sin (Rom 3:9-23; 5:12). A special use of the term *hamartolos* occurs in the Gospels and refers to those who have a reputation for being guilty of grievous sins, such as tax collectors, prostitutes, and pagans (see Mt 9:10-11; Lk 6:32-34; 7:34-39). In the aftermath of Jesus' miracle of healing the man born blind (John 9), Jewish leaders used the term *sinner* in this especially derisive sense to describe Jesus (v. 24). In doing so they hoped to undermine the clear implications of this miracle, that Jesus was the Messiah, and to keep people from following Him.

opened his eyes was a Sabbath. [15] So again the Pharisees asked him how he received his sight.

"He put mud on my eyes," he told them. "I washed and I can see."

[16] Therefore some of the Pharisees said, "This man is not from God, for He doesn't keep the Sabbath!" But others were saying, "How can a sinful man perform such signs?" And there was a division among them.

[17] Again they asked the blind man,[a] "What do you say about Him, since He opened your eyes?"

"He's a prophet," he said.

[18] The Jews did not believe this about him—that he was blind and received sight—until they summoned the parents of the one who had received his sight.

[19] They asked them, "Is this your son, whom you say was born blind? How then does he now see?"

[20] "We know this is our son and that he was born blind," his parents answered. [21] "But we don't know how he now sees, and we don't know who opened his eyes. Ask him; he's of age. He will speak for himself."

[22] His parents said these things because they were afraid of the Jews, since the Jews had already agreed that if anyone confessed Him as Messiah, he would be banned from the synagogue. [23] This is why his parents said, "He's of age; ask him."

[24] So a second time they summoned the man who had been blind and told him, "Give glory to God.[b] We know that this man is a sinner!"

[25] He answered, "Whether or not He's a sinner, I don't know. One thing I do know: I was blind, and now I can see!"

[26] Then they asked him, "What did He do to you? How did He open your eyes?"

[27] "I already told you," he said, "and you didn't listen. Why do you want to hear it again? You don't want to become His disciples too, do you?"

[28] They ridiculed him: "You're that man's disciple, but we're Moses' disciples. [29] We know that God has spoken to Moses. But this man—we don't know where He's from!"

[30] "This is an amazing thing," the man told them.

---

[a]9:17 I.e. the man who had been blind

[b]9:24 *Give glory to God* was a solemn charge to tell the truth (see Josh 7:19).

"You don't know where He is from; yet He opened my eyes! [31] We know that God doesn't listen to sinners; but if anyone is God-fearing and does His will, He listens to him. [32] Throughout history[a] no one has ever heard of someone opening the eyes of a person born blind. [33] If this man were not from God, He wouldn't be able to do anything."

[34] "You were born entirely in sin," they replied, "and are you trying to teach us?" Then they threw him out.[b]

THE BLIND MAN'S SIGHT AND THE PHARISEES' BLINDNESS

[35] When Jesus heard that they had thrown the man out, He found him and asked, "Do you believe in the Son of Man?"[1c]

[36] "Who is He, Sir, that I may believe in Him?" he asked in return.

[37] Jesus answered, "You have both seen Him and He is the One speaking with you."

[38] "I believe, Lord!" he said, and he worshiped Him.

[39] Jesus said, "I came into this world for judgment, in order that those who do not see may see and those who do see may become blind."

[40] Some of the Pharisees who were with Him heard these things and asked Him, "We aren't blind too, are we?"

[41] "If you were blind," Jesus told them, "you wouldn't have sin.[d] But now that you say, 'We see'—your sin remains.

THE IDEAL SHEPHERD

10 "I assure you:[e] Anyone who doesn't enter the sheep pen by the door, but climbs in some other way, is a thief and a robber. [2] The one who enters by the door is the shepherd of the sheep. [3] The doorkeeper opens it for him, and the sheep hear his voice. He calls his own sheep by name and leads them out. [4] When he has brought all his own outside, he goes ahead of them.

[1]9:35 Other mss read *the Son of God*

[a]9:32 Lit *From the age*
[b]9:34 I.e. they banned him from the synogogue (see v. 22).
[c]9:35 See note at 1:51
[d]9:41 *To have sin* is an idiom that refers to guilt caused by sin.
[e]10:1 See note at 1:51

Look for More Than Circumstances

Never, ever determine the truth of a situation by looking at the circumstances. Don't evaluate your situation until you have heard from Jesus. He is the Truth of all your circumstances.

He answered, "Whether or not He's a sinner, I don't know. One thing I do know: I was blind, and now I can see!"

—John 9:25

God Will Give You Everything You Need

God will never give you an assignment that He will not, at the same time, enable you to complete. That is what a spiritual gift is—a supernatural empowering to accomplish the assignment God gives you.

"If this man were not from God, He wouldn't be able to do anything."

—John 9:33

WORD STUDY

Greek word: **poimen**
[poy MAYN]
Translation: **shepherd**
Uses in John: **6**
Uses in John's writings: **6**
Uses in the NT: **18**
Key passage: **John 10:1-18**

The Greek word *poimen* occurs in John's Gospel only in John 10 where Jesus refers to Himself as "the good shepherd who lays down his life for the sheep" (v. 11). The sheep (believers) and the shepherd (Jesus) know each other, and the shepherd will bring all the sheep from the various folds (nations) into one flock (vv. 14-16).

The background for Jesus' use of the shepherd imagery is Ezekiel 34. God denounced the false shepherds (i.e. false prophets) who led the sheep (the nation of Judah) astray (vv. 1-10). Then the LORD said, "I Myself will search for My sheep, and I will seek them out" from among the many places they are scattered (vv. 11-12). Finally, David will be the shepherd over God's people again (vv. 23-24). In using the shepherd/sheep imagery, Jesus was identifying Himself as the shepherd of Israel, just as the LORD had done in this OT passage—a clear statement that Jesus claimed to be deity. Jesus also indicated that He would have the role of David as shepherd—a clear statement that Jesus claimed to be the Messiah. No wonder "a division took place among the Jews" (v. 19) at this time! Some even thought Jesus was demon possessed, but others took Jesus' claim seriously since He had healed a blind man (vv. 20-21).

The sheep follow him because they recognize his voice. [5] They will never follow a stranger; instead they will run away from him, because they don't recognize the voice of strangers."

[6] Jesus gave them this illustration, but they did not understand what He was telling them.

THE GOOD SHEPHERD

[7] So Jesus said again, "I assure you:[a] I am the door of the sheep. [8] All who came before Me are thieves and robbers, but the sheep didn't listen to them. [9] I am the door. If anyone enters by Me, he will be saved, and will come in and go out and find pasture. [10] A thief comes only to steal and to kill and to destroy. I have come that they may have life, and that they may have it in abundance.

[11] "I am the good shepherd. The good shepherd lays down His life for the sheep. [12] The hired man, since he's not the shepherd and doesn't own the sheep, leaves them[b] and runs away when he sees a wolf coming. The wolf then snatches and scatters them. [13] This happens[c] because he is a hired man and doesn't care about the sheep.

[14] "I am the good shepherd. I know My own sheep, and they know Me, [15] as the Father knows Me, and I know the Father. I lay down My life for the sheep. [16] But I have other sheep that are not of this fold; I must bring them also, and they will listen to My voice. Then there will be one flock, one shepherd. [17] This is why the Father loves Me, because I am laying down My life that I may take it up again. [18] No one takes it from Me, but I lay it down on My own. I have the right to lay it down and I have the right to take it up again. I have received this command from My Father."

[19] Again a division[d] took place among the Jews because of these words. [20] Many of them were saying, "He has a demon and He's crazy! Why do you listen to Him?" [21] Others were saying, "These aren't the words of someone demon-possessed. Can a demon open the eyes of the blind?"

---

[a] **10:7** See note at 1:51
[b] **10:12** Lit *sheep*
[c] **10:13** *This happens* added for clarity
[d] **10:19** 7:43

JESUS AT THE FESTIVAL
OF DEDICATION

22 Then the festival of Dedication[a] took place in Jerusalem; and it was winter. 23 Jesus was walking in the temple complex in Solomon's Colonnade.[b] 24 Then the Jews surrounded Him and asked, "How long are you going to keep us in suspense?[c] If You are the Messiah,[de] tell us plainly."[f]

25 "I did tell you and you don't believe," Jesus answered them. "The works that I do in My Father's name testify about Me. 26 But you don't believe because you are not My sheep.[1] 27 My sheep hear My voice, I know them, and they follow Me. 28 I give them eternal life, and they will never perish—ever! No one will snatch them out of My hand. 29 My Father, who has given them to Me, is greater than all. No one is able to snatch them out of the Father's hand. 30 The Father and I are one."[g]

RENEWED EFFORTS
TO STONE JESUS

31 Again the Jews picked up rocks to stone Him.

32 Jesus replied, "I have shown you many good works from the Father. For which of these works are you stoning Me?"

33 "We aren't stoning You for a good work," the Jews answered, "but for blasphemy, and because You—being a man—make Yourself God."

34 Jesus answered them, "Isn't it written in your law,[2] 'I said, you are gods'?[h] 35 If He called those to whom the Word of God came 'gods'—and the Scripture cannot be broken— 36 do you say, 'You are blaspheming,' to the One the Father set apart and sent into the world, because I said 'I am the Son of God'? 37 If I am not doing My Father's works, don't believe Me. 38 But if I am doing them and you don't believe Me, believe the works.

Trust Him to Speak
Where You Can Hear

God speaks to individuals, and He can do it in any way He pleases. As you walk in an intimate love relationship with God, you will come to recognize His voice. You will know when God is speaking to you.

"The sheep follow him because they recognize his voice."

—John 10:4b

---

[1] **10:26** Other mss read *not My sheep, just as I told you*
[2] **10:34** Other mss read *in the law*

---

[a] **10:22** Or *Hannukah,* also called *the feast of lights.* This festival commemorated the rededication of the temple in 164 B.C.
[b] **10:23** See note at 5:2
[c] **10:24** Lit *How long are you taking away our life?*
[d] **10:24** Or *the Christ*
[e] **10:24** See note at 1:41
[f] **10:24** Or *openly, publicly*
[g] **10:30** Lit *I and the Father—We are one.*
[h] **10:34** Ps 82:6

WORD STUDY

Greek word: **anastasis**
[ah NAH stah sihss]

Translation: **resurrection**

Uses in John's Gospel: **4**

Uses in John's writings: **6**

Uses in the NT: **42**

Key passages: **John 5:29; 11:24–
25; Rev 20:5–6**

The Greek noun *anastasis* is derived from the verb *anistemi,*
meaning literally *to stand up* and
then by extension "to rise up."
Both words could be used meta-
phorically. The word *anastasis*
was common in the ancient Greek
world, but it rarely referred to the
resurrection of the dead, which is
the dominant meaning of its occurrences in the NT. Two major
events are described with the
word *anastasis* in the NT: the
physical, bodily resurrection of
Jesus in the past (Jn 11:25; Rom
1:4; 1 Cor 15:12–13), and the
physical, bodily resurrection of
believers in the future (Jn 5:29;
11:24; 1 Cor 15:42; Phil 3:11; Rev
20:5–6).

This way you will know and understand[1] that the Father
is in Me and I in the Father." [39] Then they were trying
again to seize Him,[a] yet He eluded their grasp.

MANY BEYOND THE JORDAN BELIEVE IN JESUS

[40] So He departed again across the Jordan to the place
where John first was baptizing, and He remained there.
[41] Many came to Him and said, "John never did a sign,
but everything John said about this man was true."
[42] And many believed in Him there.

LAZARUS DIES AT BETHANY

11 A certain man was sick, Lazarus from Bethany,
the village of Mary and her sister Martha. [2] Mary
was the one who anointed the Lord with fragrant oil
and wiped His feet with her hair,[b] and it was her
brother Lazarus who was sick. [3] So the sisters sent a
message to Him: "Lord, the one You love is sick."
[4] When Jesus heard it, He said, "This sickness will not
end in death, but is for the glory of God, so that the Son
of God may be glorified through it." [5] (Jesus loved
Martha, her sister, and Lazarus.) [6] So when He heard that
he was sick, He stayed two more days in the place
where He was. [7] Then after that, He said to the disciples,
"Let's go to Judea again."

[8] "Rabbi," the disciples told Him, "just now the Jews
tried to stone You, and You're going there again?"

[9] "Aren't there twelve hours in a day?" Jesus
answered. "If anyone walks during the day, he doesn't
stumble, because he sees the light of this world. [10] If
anyone walks during the night, he does stumble,
because the light is not in him." [11] He said this, and then
He told them, "Our friend Lazarus has fallen asleep, but
I'm on My way to wake him up."

[12] Then the disciples said to Him, "Lord, if he has
fallen asleep, he will get well."

[13] Jesus, however, was speaking about his death, but
they thought He was speaking about natural sleep. [14] So
Jesus then told them plainly, "Lazarus has died. [15] I'm

---

[1]10:38 Other mss read *know and believe*

[a]10:39 7:44   [b]11:2 12:3

glad for you that I wasn't there, so that you may believe. But let's go to him."

[16] Then Thomas (called "Twin") said to his fellow disciples, "Let's go so that we may die with Him."

THE RESURRECTION
AND THE LIFE

[17] When Jesus arrived, He found that Lazarus[a] had already been in the tomb four days. [18] Bethany was near Jerusalem (about two miles[b] away). [19] Many of the Jews had come to Martha and Mary to comfort them about their brother. [20] As soon as Martha heard that Jesus was coming, she went to meet Him. But Mary remained seated in the house.

[21] Then Martha said to Jesus, "Lord, if You had been here, my brother wouldn't have died. [22] Yet even now I know that whatever You ask from God, God will give You."

[23] "Your brother will rise again," Jesus told her.

[24] Martha said, "I know that he will rise again in the resurrection at the last day."

[25] Jesus said to her, "I am the resurrection and the life. The one who believes in Me, even if he dies, will live. [26] Everyone who lives and believes in Me will never die—ever. Do you believe this?"

[27] "Yes, Lord," she told Him, "I believe You are the Messiah, the Son of God, who was to come into the world."

JESUS SHARES
THE SORROW OF DEATH

[28] Having said this, she went back and called her sister Mary, saying in private, "The Teacher is here and is calling for you."

[29] As soon as she heard this, she got up quickly and went to Him. [30] Jesus had not yet come into the village, but was still in the place where Martha had met Him. [31] The Jews who were with her in the house consoling her saw that Mary got up quickly and went out. So they followed her, supposing that she was going to the tomb to cry there.

[32] When Mary came to where Jesus was and saw Him,

Pray Expectantly

When I pray, it never crosses my mind that God is not going to answer. Expect God to answer prayer, but stick around for the answer. His timing is always right and best.

Then Martha said to Jesus, "Lord, if You had been here, my brother wouldn't have died. Yet even now I know that whatever You ask from God, God will give You."

—John 11:21–22

Repeat These Words:
"Yes, Lord."

Two words in the Christian's language cannot go together: "No, Lord." If He really is your Lord, your answer must always be "Yes."

"Yes, Lord," she told Him, "I believe You are the Messiah, the Son of God, who was to come into the world."

—John 11:27

[a]**11:17** Lit *he*   [b]**11:18** Gk *fifteen stadia*

she fell at His feet and told Him, "Lord, if You had been here, my brother would not have died!"

[33] When Jesus saw her crying, and the Jews who had come with her crying, He was angry[a] in His spirit and deeply moved. [34] "Where have you put him?" He asked.

"Lord," they told Him, "come and see."

[35] Jesus wept.

[36] So the Jews said, "See how He loved him!" [37] But some of them said, "Couldn't He who opened the blind man's eyes also have kept this man from dying?"

THE SEVENTH SIGN: RAISING LAZARUS FROM THE DEAD

[38] Then Jesus, angry[b] in Himself again, came to the tomb. It was a cave, and a stone was lying against it. [39] "Remove the stone," Jesus said.

Martha, the dead man's sister, told Him, "Lord, he already stinks. It's been four days."

[40] Jesus said to her, "Did I not tell you that if you believed you would see the glory of God?"

[41] So they removed the stone. Then Jesus raised His eyes and said, "Father, I thank You that You heard Me. [42] I know that You always hear Me, but because of the crowd standing here I said this, so they may believe You sent Me." [43] After He said this, He shouted with a loud voice, "Lazarus, come out!" [44] The dead man came out bound hand and foot with linen strips and with his face wrapped in a cloth. Jesus said to them, "Loose him and let him go."

THE PLOT TO KILL JESUS

[45] Therefore many of the Jews who came to Mary and saw what He did believed in Him. [46] But some of them went to the Pharisees and told them what Jesus had done.

[47] So the chief priests and the Pharisees convened the Sanhedrin[c] and said, "What are we going to do since this man does many signs? [48] If we let Him continue in this way, everybody will believe in Him! Then the

When You Believe, God Makes Your Life Unbelievable

Anyone who will take the time to enter into an intimate relationship with God can see God do extraordinary things through his or her life.

Jesus said to her, "Did I not tell you that if you believed you would see the glory of God?"

—John 11:40

---

[a]11:33 The Gk word is very strong and probably indicates Jesus' anger against sin's tyranny and death.
[b]11:38 See note at v. 33.

[c]11:47 The Jewish council in Jerusalem with religious, civil, and criminal authority

Romans will come and remove both our place[a] and our nation."

[49] One of them, Caiaphas, who was high priest that year, said to them, "You know nothing at all! [50] You're not considering that it is to your advantage that one man should die for the people rather than the whole nation perish." [51] He did not say this on his own; but being high priest that year he prophesied that Jesus was going to die for the nation, [52] and not for the nation only, but also to unite the scattered children of God. [53] So from that day on they plotted to kill Him. [54] Therefore Jesus no longer walked openly among the Jews, but departed from there to the countryside near the wilderness, to a town called Ephraim. And He stayed there with the disciples.

[55] Now the Jewish Passover was near, and before the Passover many went up to Jerusalem from the country to purify[b] themselves. [56] They were looking for Jesus, and asking one another as they stood in the temple complex: "What do you think? He won't come to the festival, will He?"

[57] The chief priests and the Pharisees had given orders that if anyone knew where He was, he should report it so they could arrest Him.

THE ANOINTING AT BETHANY

12 Six days before the Passover, Jesus came to Bethany where Lazarus was, whom Jesus had raised from the dead. [2] So they gave a dinner for Him there; Martha was serving them, and Lazarus was one of those reclining at the table with Him. [3] Then Mary took a pound of fragrant oil—pure and expensive nard— anointed Jesus' feet, and wiped His feet with her hair. So the house was filled with the fragrance of the oil.

[4] Then one of His disciples, Judas Iscariot (who was about to betray Him), said, [5] "Why wasn't this fragrant oil sold for three hundred denarii[c] and given to the poor?" [6] He didn't say this because he cared about the poor, but because he was a thief. He was in charge of

Your First Priority: Love Him

Can you describe your relationship with God by sincerely saying, "I love You with all my heart"?

Then Mary took a pound of fragrant oil—pure and expensive nard—anointed Jesus' feet, and wiped His feet with her hair.

—John 12:3

---

[a]11:48 The temple or possibly all of Jerusalem
[b]11:55 The law of Moses required God's people to purify or cleanse themselves so they could celebrate the Passover. Jews often came to Jerusalem a week early to do this (Num 9:4–11).
[c]12:5 This amount was about a year's wages for a common worker.

the money bag and would steal part of what was put in it.

⁷ Jesus answered, "Leave her alone; she has kept it for the day of My burial. ⁸ For you always have the poor with you, but you do not always have Me."

THE DECISION TO KILL LAZARUS

⁹ Then a large crowd of the Jews learned that He was there. They came not only because of Jesus, but also to see Lazarus whom He had raised from the dead. ¹⁰ Therefore the chief priests decided to kill Lazarus too, ¹¹ because he was the reason many of the Jews were deserting them[a] and believing in Jesus.

THE TRIUMPHAL ENTRY

¹² The next day, when the large crowd that had come to the festival heard that Jesus was coming to Jerusalem, ¹³ they took palm branches and went out to meet Him. They kept shouting: **"Hosanna![b] 'Blessed is He who comes in the name of the Lord'[c]**—the King of Israel!"

¹⁴ Jesus found a young donkey and mounted it, just as it is written: ¹⁵ **"Fear no more, Daughter of Zion; look! your King is coming, sitting on a donkey's colt."[d]**

¹⁶ His disciples did not understand these things at first. However when Jesus was glorified, then they remembered that these things had been written about Him and that they had done these things to Him. ¹⁷ Meanwhile the crowd, which had been with Him when He called Lazarus out of the tomb and raised him from the dead, continued to testify. ¹⁸ This is also why the crowd met Him, because they heard He had done this sign.

¹⁹ Then the Pharisees said to one another, "You see? You've accomplished nothing. Look—the world has gone after Him!"

JESUS PREDICTS HIS CRUCIFIXION

²⁰ Now there were some Greeks among those who went up to worship at the festival. ²¹ So they came to

---

God's Will Is an Expensive Calling

You cannot know and do the will of God without paying the price of adjustment and obedience.

"I assure you: Unless a grain of wheat falls into the ground and dies, it remains by itself. But if it dies, it produces a large crop."

—John 12:24

---

[a]**12:11** Lit *going away*
[b]**12:13** *Hosanna* is a term of praise derived from the Hb word for *save* (see Ps 118:25).
[c]**12:13** Ps 118:25–26
[d]**12:15** Zch 9:9

Philip, who was from Bethsaida in Galilee, and requested of him, "Sir, we want to see Jesus."

²² Philip went and told Andrew; then Andrew and Philip went and told Jesus. ²³ Jesus replied to them, "The hour has come for the Son of Man to be glorified.

²⁴ "I assure you:ᵃ Unless a grain of wheat falls into the ground and dies, it remains by itself. But if it dies, it produces a large crop.ᵇ ²⁵ The one who loves his life will lose it, and the one who hates his life in this world will keep it for eternal life. ²⁶ If anyone serves Me, he must follow Me. Where I am, there My servant also will be. If anyone serves Me, the Father will honor him.

²⁷ "Now My soul is troubled. What should I say— 'Father, save Me from this hour'? But that is why I came to this hour. ²⁸ Father, glorify Your name!"

Then a voice came from heaven: "I have glorified it, and I will glorify it again!"

²⁹ The crowd standing there heard it and said it was thunder. Others said, "An angel has spoken to Him!"

³⁰ Jesus responded, "This voice came, not for Me, but for you. ³¹ Now is the judgment of this world. Now the ruler of this world will be cast out. ³² As for Me, if I am lifted upᶜ from the earth I will draw all peopleᵈ to Myself." ³³ He said this to signify what kind of death He was about to die.

³⁴ Then the crowd replied to Him, "We have heard from the law that the Messiah would remain forever.ᵉ So how can You say, 'The Son of Man must be lifted up'?ᶠ Who is this Son of Man?"

³⁵ Jesus answered, "The light will be with you only a little longer. Walk while you have the light, so that darkness doesn't overtake you. The one who walks in darkness doesn't know where he's going. ³⁶ While you have the light, believe in the light, so that you may become sons of light." Jesus said this, then went away and hid from them.

ISAIAH'S PROPHECIES FULFILLED

³⁷ Even though He had performed so many signs in their presence, they did not believe in Him. ³⁸ But this was to fulfill the word of Isaiah the prophet, who said:ᵍ

ᵃ**12:24** See note at 1:51
ᵇ**12:24** Lit *much fruit*
ᶜ**12:32** Or *exalted*
ᵈ**12:32** *people* is implied from the context
ᶜ**12:34** Ps 89:36
ᶠ**12:34** Or *exalted*
ᵍ**12:38** Lit *which he said*

What You Do Will Reveal Who You Are

You cannot stay where you are and go with God. You cannot continue doing things your way and accomplish God's purposes in His ways.

"If anyone serves Me, he must follow Me. Where I am, there My servant also will be. If anyone serves Me, the Father will honor him."

—John 12:26

Keep Your Focus on Today

God always will give you enough specific directions to do *now* what He wants you to do. When you need more directions, He gives you more in His timing.

Jesus answered, "The light will be with you only a little longer. Walk while you have the light, so that darkness doesn't overtake you. The one who walks in darkness doesn't know where he's going."

—John 12:35

WORD STUDY

Greek word: *doxa* [DAHKS uh]

Translation: **glory, praise**

Uses in John's Gospel: **19**

Uses in John's writings: **36**

Uses in the NT: **166**

Key passage: **John 12:41-43**

The use of *doxa (glory)* in the NT is shaped by the Hebrew word *kabod* that is so common in the OT. The noun *kabod* is derived from a Hebrew verb meaning *to be heavy.* (A related noun, *kebed,* means *liver,* the heavy organ.) Thus, to recognize the glory of something is to attach weight or importance to it. The glory of the Lord refers to His nature and holiness as manifested to His creatures, humans and angels, both of whom can share in that glory. Even in the incarnation, Jesus shared in the Father's glory and especially manifested His grace and truth (Jn 1:14; see 17:5). The greatest manifestation of God's glory happened at the cross (Jn 13:31-32; the related verb *doxazo* [*glorify*] is used here), for here God's greatest work occurred. We praise God when we give Him glory, acknowledging that He is of greatest importance to us. Thus, *doxa* may often mean *praise.* John 12 contains a word play with these two meanings. John stated that Isaiah saw God's glory, which refers to the prophet's vision of the LORD in the temple with the Seraphs exclaiming: "Holy! Holy! Holy! is the LORD of Hosts! His glory fills the whole earth!" (Isa 6:3). But according to John, Isaiah saw the glory *(doxa)* of Jesus (v. 41). Those who refused to confess Him did so because "they loved praise [*doxa*] from men more than praise [*doxa*] from God" (v. 43).

> Lord, who has believed our report?
> And to whom has the arm of the Lord been revealed?[a]

[39] This is why they were unable to believe, because Isaiah also said:

> [40] He has blinded their eyes
> And hardened their hearts,[b]
> So that they would not see with their eyes
> Or understand with their hearts,
> And be converted,
> And I would heal them.[c]

[41] Isaiah said these things because[1] he saw His glory and spoke about Him.

[42] Nevertheless, many did believe in Him even among the rulers, but because of the Pharisees they did not confess Him, so they would not be banned from the synagogue. [43] For they loved praise from men more than praise[d] from God.

A SUMMARY OF JESUS' MISSION

[44] Then Jesus cried out, "The one who believes in Me believes not in Me, but in Him who sent Me. [45] And the one who sees Me sees Him who sent Me. [46] I have come as a light into the world, so that everyone who believes in Me would not remain in darkness. [47] If anyone hears My words and doesn't keep them, I do not judge him; for I did not come to judge the world, but to save the world. [48] The one who rejects Me and doesn't accept My sayings has this as his judge:[e] the word I have spoken will judge him on the last day. [49] For I have not spoken on My own, but the Father Himself who sent Me has given Me a command as to what I should say and what I should speak. [50] I know that His command is eternal life. So the things that I speak, I speak just as the Father has told Me."

[1]12:41 Other mss read *when*

[a]12:38 Isa 53:1
[b]12:40 Lit *heart* (both times)
[c]12:40 Isa 6:10

[d]12:43 Lit *glory from men . . . glory from God;* see v. 41; 5:41
[e]12:48 Lit *has the one judging him*

JESUS WASHES
HIS DISCIPLES' FEET

13 Before the Passover festival, Jesus knew that His hour had come to depart from this world to the Father. Having loved His own who were in the world, He loved them to the end.[a]

[2] Now by the time of supper, the Devil had already put it into the heart of Judas, Simon Iscariot's son, to betray Him. [3] Jesus knew that the Father had given everything into His hands, that He had come from God, and that He was going back to God. [4] So He got up from supper, laid aside His robe, took a towel, and tied it around Himself. [5] Next, He poured water into a basin and began to wash His disciples' feet and to dry them with the towel tied around Him.

[6] He came to Simon Peter, who asked Him, "Lord, are You going to wash my feet?"

[7] Jesus answered him, "What I'm doing you don't understand now, but afterward you will know."

[8] "You will never wash my feet—ever!" Peter said.

Jesus replied, "If I don't wash you, you have no part with Me."

[9] Simon Peter said to Him, "Lord, not only my feet, but also my hands and my head."

[10] "One who has bathed," Jesus told him, "doesn't need to wash anything except his feet, but he is completely clean. You are clean, but not all of you." [11] For He knew who would betray Him. This is why He said, "You are not all clean."

THE MEANING OF FOOTWASHING

[12] When Jesus had washed their feet and put on His robe, He reclined[b] again and said to them, "Do you know what I have done for you? [13] You call Me Teacher and Lord. This is well said, for I am. [14] So if I, your Lord and Teacher, have washed your feet, you also ought to wash one another's feet. [15] For I have given you an example that you also should do just as I have done for you.

[16] "I assure you:[c] A slave is not greater than his

WORD STUDY

Greek word: ***didaskalos***
[dih DAHSS kuh lahss]
Translation: **teacher**
Uses in John: **8**
Uses in John's writings: **8**
Uses in the NT: **59**
Key passage: **John 13:13–14**

The Greek word *didaskalos* refers to Jesus most of the time in the Gospels but never does outside the Gospels. In the Gospels the term is used of a recognized spiritual leader with a group of committed followers or disciples (see word study on *mathetes* on page 40). John used *didaskalos* as the Greek equivalent of the technical Hebrew term *rabbi* (see note at 1:38) and the corresponding Aramaic term *rabbouni* (see note at 20:16). The teacher not only instructed people about the Word of God but in so doing challenged them to conform to its demands. Jesus did this better than anyone else; thus, the majority of times *didaskalos* refers to Jesus in the Gospels, it is used as a title ("Teacher"). So strong was the role of the teacher in the life of a disciple that Jesus connected it with His title as "Lord" (Jn 13:13–14).

---

[a]**13:1** *to the end* can mean *completely* or *always*
[b]**13:12** At important meals the custom was to recline on a mat at a low table and lean on the left elbow.
[c]**13:16** See note at 1:51

WORD STUDY

Greek word: **mathetes**
[mah thay TAYSS]

Translation: **disciple**

Uses in John: **78**

Uses in John's writings: **78**

Uses in the NT: **261**

Key passage: **John 13:35**

The English word *disciple* basically means *follower*. The Greek word *mathetes,* however, comes from the verb *manthano,* which means *to learn.* Thus, a *mathetes* is primarily a learner, though being a follower is certainly included also. *Mathetes* occurs only in the Gospels and Acts and refers to disciples of various teachers or rabbis, such as the Pharisees (Mk 2:18) and John the Baptist (Jn 1:35). In Jewish life there was no such thing as a *mathetes* without a *didaskalos* (*teacher,* see word study on *didaskalos* on page 39), the one the disciple learned from. Most often in the NT *mathetes* refers to disciples of Jesus, sometimes in general (Jn 6:61,66) but most often to the Twelve. Jesus stated that the single attribute that characterizes His disciples is that they love one another (Jn 13:35).

master,[ab] and a messenger is not greater than the one who sent him. [17] If you know these things, you are blessed if you do them. [18] I'm not speaking about all of you; I know those I have chosen.[c] But the Scripture must be fulfilled: **'The one who eats My bread[1] has raised his heel against Me.'**[d]

[19] "I am telling you now before it happens, so that when it does happen you will believe that I am He.[e] [20] I assure you:[f] The one who receives whomever I send receives Me, and the one who receives Me receives Him who sent Me."

JUDAS' BETRAYAL PREDICTED

[21] When Jesus had said this, He was troubled in His spirit and testified, "I assure you:[f] One of you will betray Me!"

[22] The disciples started looking at one another—at a loss as to which one He was speaking about. [23] One of His disciples, whom Jesus loved,[g] was reclining close beside Jesus.[h] [24] Simon Peter motioned to him to find out who it was He was talking about. [25] So he leaned back against Jesus and asked Him, "Lord, who is it?"

[26] Jesus replied, "He's the one I give the piece of bread to after I have dipped it." When He had dipped the bread, He gave it to Judas, Simon Iscariot's son.[2] [27] After Judas ate[i] the piece of bread, Satan entered him. Therefore Jesus told him, "What you're doing, do quickly."

[28] None of those reclining at the table knew why He told him this. [29] Since Judas kept the money bag, some thought that Jesus was telling him, "Buy what we need for the festival," or that he should give something to the poor. [30] After receiving the piece of bread, he went out immediately. And it was night.

THE NEW COMMANDMENT

[31] When he had gone out, Jesus said, "Now the Son of Man is glorified, and God is glorified in Him. [32] If God is

[1]**13:18** Other mss read *eats bread with Me*
[2]**13:26** Other mss read *Judas Iscariot, Simon's son*

---

[a]**13:16** Or *lord*
[b]**13:16** 15:20
[c]**13:18** 6:70
[d]**13:18** Ps 41:9
[e]**13:19** Lit *I am;* see note at 8:58

[f]**13:20, 21** See note at 1:51
[g]**13:23** 11:5; 19:26; 20:2; 21:7,20
[h]**13:23** Lit *reclining at Jesus' breast;*
i.e. on His right; see 1:18
[i]**13:27** *Judas ate* added for clarity

glorified in Him,[1] God will also glorify Him in Himself, and will glorify Him at once.

[33] "Children, I am with you a little while longer. You will look for Me, and just as I told the Jews, 'Where I am going you cannot come,' so now I tell you.

[34] "I give you a new commandment: that you love one another. Just as I have loved you, you should also love one another. [35] By this all people will know that you are My disciples, if you have love for one another."

PETER'S DENIALS PREDICTED

[36] "Lord," Simon Peter said to Him, "where are You going?"

Jesus answered, "Where I am going you cannot follow Me now; but you will follow later."

[37] "Lord," Peter asked, "why can't I follow You now? I will lay down my life for You!"

[38] Jesus replied, "Will you lay down your life for Me? I assure you:[a] A rooster will not crow until you have denied Me three times.

THE WAY TO THE FATHER

14 "Your heart must not be troubled. Believe in God; believe also in Me.[b] [2] In My Father's house are many homes;[c] if not, I would have told you. I[2] am going away to prepare a place for you. [3] If I go away and prepare a place for you, I will come back and receive you to Myself, so that where I am you may be also. [4] You know the way where I am going."[3]

[5] "Lord," Thomas said, "we don't know where You're going. How can we know the way?"

[6] Jesus told him, "I am the way, the truth, and the life. No one comes to the Father except through Me.

---

[1]**13:32** Other mss omit *If God is glorified in Him*
[2]**14:2** Other mss read *For I*
[3]**14:4** Other mss read this verse as *And you know where I am going, and you know the way*

---

[a]**13:38** See note at 1:51
[b]**14:1** Or *You believe in God; believe also in Me*
[c]**14:2** The Vulgate used the Latin term *mansio*, a traveler's resting place. The Gk word is related to the verb *meno*, meaning *remain* or *stay*, which occurs forty times in John.

Expect Times of Testing and Stretching

Waiting on the Lord should not be an idle time for you. Let God use times of waiting to mold and shape your character. Let God use those times to purify your life and make you into a clean vessel for His service.

"Lord," Peter asked, "why can't I follow You now? I will lay down my life for You!" Jesus replied, "Will you lay down your life for Me? I assure you: A rooster will not crow until you have denied Me three times."

—John 13:37–38

JESUS REVEALS THE FATHER

[7] "If you know Me, you will also know[1] My Father. From now on you do know Him and have seen Him."

[8] "Lord," said Philip, "show us the Father, and that's enough for us."

[9] Jesus said to him, "Have I been among you all this time without you knowing Me, Philip? The one who has seen Me has seen the Father. How can you say, 'Show us the Father'? [10] Don't you believe that I am in the Father and the Father is in Me?[a] The words I speak to you I do not speak on My own. The Father who lives in Me does His works. [11] Believe Me that I am in the Father and the Father is in Me. Otherwise, believe[2] because of the works themselves.

PRAYING IN JESUS' NAME

[12] "I assure you:[b] The one who believes in Me will also do the works that I do. And he will do even greater works than these, because I am going to the Father. [13] Whatever you ask in My name, I will do it, so that the Father may be glorified in the Son. [14] If you ask Me[3] anything in My name, I will do it.

ANOTHER COUNSELOR PROMISED

[15] "If you love Me, you will keep[4] My commandments; [16] and I also will ask the Father, and He will give you another Counselor[c] to be with you forever. [17] He is the Spirit of truth, whom the world is unable to receive because it doesn't see Him or know Him. But you do know Him, because He remains with you and will be[5] in you. [18] I will not leave you as orphans; I am coming to you.

You'd Be Surprised What He Can Do Through You

I have come to the place in my life that, if the assignment I sense God is giving me is something that I know I can handle, I know it probably is not from God.

"I assure you: The one who believes in Me will also do the works that I do. And he will do even greater works than these, because I am going to the Father."

—John 14:12

The Holy Spirit Will Steer You Right

When the Holy Spirit reveals Truth, He is not teaching you a concept to be thought about. He is leading you to a relationship with a Person.

"But the Counselor, the Holy Spirit, whom the Father will send in My name, will teach you all things and remind you of everything I have told you."

—John 14:26

---

[1] **14:7** Other mss read *If you had known Me, you would have known*
[2] **14:11** Other mss read *believe Me*
[3] **14:14** Other mss omit *Me*
[4] **14:15** Many mss read *If you love Me, keep* (a command)
[5] **14:17** Other mss read *is*

---

[a] **14:10** 10:30,38
[b] **14:12** See note at 1:51
[c] **14:16** Gk *Parakletos,* one called alongside to help, counsel, or protect (see v. 26; 15:26; 16:7; 1 Jn 2:1)

THE FATHER, THE SON, AND THE HOLY SPIRIT

[19] "In a little while the world will see Me no longer, but you will see Me. Because I live, you will live too. [20] In that day you will know that I am in My Father, you are in Me, and I am in you. [21] The one who has My commandments and keeps them is the one who loves Me. And the one who loves Me will be loved by My Father. I also will love him and will reveal Myself to him."

[22] Judas (not Iscariot) said to him, "Lord, how is it You're going to reveal Yourself to us and not to the world?"

[23] Jesus answered, "If anyone loves Me, he will keep My word. My Father will love him, and We will come to him and make Our home with him. [24] The one who doesn't love Me will not keep My words. The word that you hear is not Mine, but is from the Father who sent Me.

[25] "I have spoken these things to you while I remain with you. [26] But the Counselor, the Holy Spirit, whom the Father will send in My name, will teach you all things and remind you of everything I have told you.

JESUS' GIFT OF PEACE

[27] "Peace I leave with you. My peace I give to you. I do not give to you as the world gives. Your heart must not be troubled or fearful. [28] You have heard me tell you, 'I am going away and I am coming to you.' If you loved Me, you would have rejoiced that I am going to the Father, because the Father is greater than I. [29] I have told you now before it happens, so that when it does happen you may believe. [30] I will not talk with you much longer, because the ruler of the world[a] is coming. He has no power over Me.[b] [31] On the contrary, I am going away[c] so that the world may know that I love the Father. Just as the Father commanded Me, so I do.

"Get up; let's leave this place.

THE VINE AND THE BRANCHES

15 "I am the true vine, and My Father is the vineyard keeper. [2] Every branch in Me that does not produce fruit He removes, and He prunes every branch that produces fruit so that it will produce more fruit.

---

[a]**14:30** 12:31
[b]**14:30** Lit *he has nothing in Me*

[c]**14:31** *I am going away* added for clarity and refers to the cross

WORD STUDY

Greek word: ***parakletos***
[pah RAH klay tahss]
Translation: **Counselor**
Uses in John: **4**
Uses in John's writings: **5**
Uses in the NT: **5**
Key passages: **John 14:16,26; 15:26; 16:7; 1 Jn 2:1**

The Greek word *parakletos* is derived from the verb *parakaleo* (literally *to call alongside;* basically *to comfort, counsel, exhort*). It is also related to the noun *paraklesis (comfort, exhortation).* Both are much more common than *parakletos* but do not occur in John's writings, while *parakletos* occurs only in John's writings. In all four occurrences of *parakletos* in John's Gospel, Jesus used the term to refer to the Holy Spirit as our *Counselor.* The idea is that the Spirit comes alongside to aid us in the tasks Jesus gave us as His disciples.

WORD STUDY

Greek word: **meno** [MEHN oh]
Translation: **remain**
Uses in John's Gospel: **40**
Uses in John's writings: **68**
Uses in the NT: **118**
Key passage: **John 15:1-16**

The Greek verb *meno* is commonly used in the NT to mean *remain* or *stay,* such as someone staying in a specific location (Mt 26:38; Jn 1:38-39), town (Jn 7:9; Acts 9:43), or house (Mt 10:11; Lk 19:5). John's Gospel often uses the term with a spiritual significance referring to some aspect of our relationship to God, and this is always the case for the twenty-four occurrences of *meno* in 1 John. In this spiritual sense, *meno* refers to clinging to a relationship already begun or continuing a process already started. The most concentrated use of *meno* in John's Gospel occurs in John 15:1-16 (eleven times), where Jesus admonished the disciples to always cling to Him so that they can produce spiritual fruit. Not clinging to Jesus is costly (v. 6).

³ You are already clean because of the word I have spoken to you. ⁴ Remain in Me, and I in you. Just as a branch is unable to produce fruit by itself unless it remains on the vine, so neither can you unless you remain in Me.

⁵ "I am the vine; you are the branches. The one who remains in Me and I in him produces much fruit, because you can do nothing without Me. ⁶ If anyone does not remain in Me, he is thrown aside like a branch and he withers. They gather them, throw them into the fire, and they are burned. ⁷ If you remain in Me and My words remain in you, ask whatever you want and it will be done for you. ⁸ My Father is glorified by this: that you produce much fruit and prove to be[a] My disciples.

CHRISTLIKE LOVE

⁹ "Just as the Father has loved Me, I also have loved you. Remain in My love. ¹⁰ If you keep My commandments you will remain in My love, just as I have kept My Father's commandments and remain in His love.

¹¹ "I have spoken these things to you so that My joy may be in you and your joy may be complete. ¹² This is My commandment: that you love one another just as I have loved you. ¹³ No one has greater love than this, that someone would lay down his life for his friends. ¹⁴ You are My friends, if you do what I command you. ¹⁵ I do not call you slaves anymore, because a slave doesn't know what his master[b] is doing. I have called you friends, because I have made known to you everything I have heard from My Father. ¹⁶ You did not choose Me, but I chose you. I appointed you that you should go out and produce fruit, and that your fruit should remain, so that whatever you ask the Father in My name, He will give you. ¹⁷ This is what I command you: that you love one another.

PERSECUTIONS PREDICTED

¹⁸ "If the world hates you, understand that it hated Me before it hated you. ¹⁹ If you were of the world, the world would love you as[c] its own. However, because you are not of the world, but I have chosen you out of

---

[a]**15:8** Or *and become*
[b]**15:15** Or *lord*
[c]**15:19** *you as* added for clarity

the world, this is why the world hates you. [20] Remember the word I spoke to you: 'A slave is not greater than his master.'[ab] If they persecuted Me, they will also persecute you. If they kept My word, they will also keep yours. [21] But they will do all these things to you on account of My name, because they don't know the One who sent Me. [22] If I had not come and spoken to them, they would not have sin.[c] Now they have no excuse for their sin. [23] The one who hates Me also hates My Father. [24] If I had not done the works among them that no one else has done, they would not have sin.[c] Now they have seen and hated both Me and My Father. [25] But this happened[d] so that the statement[e] written in their law might be fulfilled:[f] **'They hated me for no reason.'**[g]

COMING TESTIMONY
AND REJECTION

[26] "When the Counselor comes, whom I will send to you from the Father—the Spirit of truth who proceeds from the Father—He will testify about Me. [27] You also will testify, because you have been with Me from the beginning.

16 "I have told you these things to keep you from stumbling. [2] They will ban[h] you from the synagogues. In fact, a time[i] is coming when anyone who kills you will think he is offering service to God. [3] They will do these things because they haven't known the Father or Me. [4] But I have told you these things so that when their time[j] comes you may remember I told them to you. I didn't tell you these things from the beginning, because I was with you.

THE COUNSELOR'S MINISTRY

[5] "But now I am going away to Him who sent Me, and not one of you asks Me, 'Where are you going?' [6] Yet, because I have spoken these things to you, sorrow has filled your heart. [7] Nevertheless, I am telling you the truth. It is for your benefit that I go away, because if I don't go away the Counselor will not come to you. If I

**Remember Where
Your Strength Lies**

Jesus realized that He could do nothing by Himself. Yet with the Father at work in Him, He could do anything. If Jesus was that dependent on the Father, then you and I should realize we are even more dependent on God the Father to be working in and through us.

"I am the vine; you are the branches. The one who remains in Me and I in him produces much fruit, because you can do nothing without Me."

—John 15:5

**Do You Know How
Much God Loves You?**

God is far more interested in a love relationship with you than He is in what you can do for Him.

"Just as the Father has loved Me, I also have loved you. Remain in My love."

—John 15:9

---

[a]**15:20** Or *lord*
[b]**15:20** 13:16
[c]**15:22, 24** See note at 9:41
[d]**15:25** *this happened* added for clarity
[e]**15:25** Lit *word*

[f]**15:25** 12:38; 13:18; 17:12; 18:9, 32; 19:24,36
[g]**15:25** Ps 69:4
[h]**16:2** 9:22; 12:42
[i]**16:2** Lit *an hour*
[j]**16:4** Lit *hour*

WORD STUDY

Greek word: **kosmos**
[KAHZ mahss]
Translation: **world**
Uses in John's Gospel: **78**
Uses in John's writings: **105**
Uses in the NT: **186**
Key passages: **John 1:10; 3:16; 16:11,28,33; 1 John 2:15–17**

The noun *kosmos* (English *cosmos, cosmic*), normally translated *world* and most often having negative connotations, especially in John's writings. John provides the foundational verse about the *kosmos* in the first chapter: "He [the Word] was in the world [earth; see 16:28], and the world [the universe; see 17:5] was created through Him, yet the world [unbelieving humanity] did not know Him" (v. 10; see 17:25). The *kosmos* is consistently described by John as hostile to Jesus and the things of God. The world needs the light (1:9; see 8:12) because it is in darkness (3:19). It is dead and needs life (6:33,51). The world hates Jesus (7:7) and His followers (15:18; 17:14), but it will be judged (9:39; 12:31), as will its prince (i.e. Satan; 12:31; 16:11). But as "the Lamb of God, who takes away the sin of the world" (1:29), Jesus "conquered the world" (16:33). God loved the world (despite its sins) and gave His Son to redeem the world (3:16–17). John warned believers not to love the world, for it is contrary to the things of God and is destined to disappear (1 Jn 2:15–17). This will occur when Jesus returns and "the kingdom of the world has become the kingdom of our Lord and of His Messiah," who "will reign forever and ever" (Rev 11:15).

go, I will send Him to you. [8] When He comes, He will convict the world about sin, righteousness, and judgment: [9] about sin, because they do not believe in Me; [10] about righteousness, because I am going to the Father[a] and you will no longer see Me; [11] and about judgment, because the ruler of this world has been judged.

[12] "I still have many things to tell you, but you can't bear them now. [13] When the Spirit of truth comes, He will guide you into all the truth. For He will not speak on His own, but He will speak whatever He hears. He will also declare to you what is to come. [14] He will glorify Me, because He will take from what is Mine and declare it to you. [15] Everything the Father has is Mine. This is why I told you that He takes from what is Mine and will declare it to you.

SORROW TURNED TO JOY

[16] "A little while and you will no longer see Me; again a little while and you will see Me."[1]

[17] Therefore some of His disciples said to one another, "What is this He tells us: 'A little while and you will not see Me; again a little while and you will see Me'; and, 'because I am going to the Father'?" [18] They said, "What is this He is saying, 'A little while'? We don't know what He's talking about!"

[19] Jesus knew they wanted to question Him, so He said to them, "Are you asking one another about what I said, 'A little while and you will not see Me; again a little while and you will see Me'?

[20] "I assure you:[b] You will weep and wail, but the world will rejoice. You will become sorrowful, but your sorrow will turn to joy. [21] When a woman is in labor she has pain because her time[c] has come. But when she has given birth to a child, she no longer remembers the suffering because of the joy that a person has been born into the world. [22] So you also have sorrow now. But I will see you again. Your hearts will rejoice, and no one will rob you of your joy. [23] In that day you will not ask Me anything.

"I assure you:[d] Anything you ask the Father in My

[1]16:16 Other mss add *because I am going to the Father*

[a]16:10 14:12,28; 15:11; 16:17   [c]16:21 Lit *hour*
[b]16:20 See note at 1:51   [d]16:23 See note at 1:51

name, He will give you.[a] [24] Until now you have asked for nothing in My name. Ask and you will receive, that your joy may be complete.

JESUS THE VICTOR

[25] "I have spoken these things to you in figures of speech. A time[b] is coming when I will no longer speak to you in figures, but I will tell you plainly about the Father. [26] In that day you will ask in My name. I am not telling you that I will make requests to the Father on your behalf. [27] For the Father Himself loves you, because you have loved Me and have believed that I came from God.[1] [28] I came from the Father and have come into the world. Again, I am leaving the world and going to the Father."

[29] "Ah!" His disciples said. "Now You're speaking plainly and not using any figurative language. [30] Now we know that You know everything and don't need anyone to question You. By this we believe that You came from God."

[31] Jesus responded to them, "Do you now believe? [32] Look: An hour is coming, and has come, when you will be scattered each to his own home, and you will leave Me alone. Yet I am not alone, because the Father is with Me. [33] I have told you these things so that in Me you may have peace. In the world you have suffering. But take courage! I have conquered the world."

JESUS PRAYS FOR HIMSELF

17 Jesus spoke these things, then raised His eyes to heaven, and said:

"Father, the hour has come.
Glorify Your Son so that the Son may glorify You,
[2] just as[c] You gave Him authority over all flesh;[d]
so that He may give eternal life to all You have given Him.

[1] 16:27 Other mss read *from the Father*

---

[a] 16:23 14:13–14; 15:16   [c] 17:2 Or *since*
[b] 16:25 Lit *an hour*   [d] 17:2 Or *people*

WORD STUDY

Greek word: **hora** [HOH rah]
Translation: **hour**
Uses in John: **26**
Uses in John's writings: **38**
Uses in the NT: **106**
Key passages: **John 2:4; 17:1**

The Greek word *hora* seldom if ever refers to a period of sixty minutes in the NT. Even "one hour" in Revelation (17:12; 18:10,17,19) should be understood as an idiom meaning *quickly* or *suddenly*. In John's Gospel a special use of *hour* occurs several times and refers to Jesus' death, though His exaltation in glory is often in view also. This meaning of *hour* first occurs at Jesus' miracle of changing the water into wine (2:4), and the final one occurs at the beginning of Jesus' prayer to the Father (17:1) just before His arrest (18:12; for others during passion week, see 12:23,27; 13:1). In between these two events, John's Gospel states on two occasions that the hour of Jesus' death had not yet arrived (7:30; 8:20). The appointed moment for His death on our behalf was set in eternity past and could not have been changed by anyone, no matter how powerful.

³ This is eternal life: that they may know You, the
   only true God,
and the One You have sent—Jesus Christ.ᵃ
⁴ I have glorified You on the earth
by completing the work You gave Me to do.
⁵ Now, Father, glorify Me in Your presence
with that glory I had with You before the world
   existed.

JESUS PRAYS FOR HIS DISCIPLES

⁶ "I have revealed Your name to the men You
   gave Me from the world.
They were Yours, You gave them to Me,
and they have kept Your word.
⁷ Now they know that all things You have given
   to Me are from You,
⁸ because the words which You gave to Me, I
   have given to them.
They have received them and have known for
   certain that I came from You.
They have believed that You sent Me.
⁹ I prayᵇ for them. I am not praying for the
   world,
but for those You have given Me,
because they are Yours.
¹⁰ All My things are Yours, and Yours are Mine,
and I have been glorified in them.
¹¹ I am no longer in the world, but they are in the
   world,
and I am coming to You.
Holy Father, protectᶜ them by Your name
that You have given Me,[1]
so that they may be one just as We are.
¹² While I was with them I was protecting them
by Your name that You have given me.[2]
I guarded them and not one of them is lost,
   except the son of destruction,ᵈ
that the Scripture may be fulfilled.ᵉ

---

[1] **17:11** Other mss read *protect them by Your name those You have given to Me*
[2] **17:12** Other mss read *I was protecting them in Your name. I guarded them, those you have given Me*

ᵃ**17:3** 5:38; 6:29
ᵇ**17:9** Lit *ask* (throughout this passage)
ᶜ**17:11** Lit *keep* (throughout this passage)

ᵈ**17:12** I.e. the one destined for destruction, loss, or perdition.
ᵉ**17:12** Ps 41:9; see Jn 13:18; 15:25; 19:24,36

¹³ Now I am coming to You, and I speak these
things in the world so that they may have My
joy completed in them.
¹⁴ I have given them Your word.
The world hated them because they are not of
the world,
just as I am not of the world.
¹⁵ I am not praying that You take them out of the
world,
but that You protect them from the evil one.
¹⁶ They are not of the world, just as I am not of
the world.
¹⁷ Sanctify[a] them by the truth; Your word is truth.
¹⁸ Just as You sent Me into the world,
I also have sent them into the world.
¹⁹ I sanctify Myself for them,
so they also may be sanctified by the truth.

JESUS PRAYS
FOR ALL BELIEVERS

²⁰ "I pray not only for these, but also for those
who believe in Me through their message.[b]
²¹ May they all be one, just as You, Father,
are in Me and I am in You.
May they also be one[1] in Us,
so that the world may believe You sent Me.
²² I have given them the glory that You have given
to Me.
May they be one just as We are one.
²³ I am in them and You are in Me.
May they be made completely one,
so that the world may know You sent Me
and that You have loved them just as You have
loved Me.
²⁴ Father, I desire those You have given Me to be
with Me where I am.
Then they may see My glory which You have
given Me,
because You loved Me before the world's
foundation.

[1] 17:21 Other mss omit *one*

---

[a] 17:17 I.e. set apart for special use   [b] 17:20 Lit *word*

God Has Put You Here for a Reason

What you plan to do for God is not important. What He plans to do where you are is very important.

"Just as You sent Me into the world, I also have sent them into the world."

—John 17:18

Your Calling Is No Better, No Worse—It Is Your Part in the Body

All members of the body belong to each other, and they need each other.

"May they all be one, just as You, Father, are in Me and I am in You. May they also be one in Us, so that the world may believe You sent Me."

—John 17:21

WORD STUDY

Greek words: **ego eimi**
[eh GOH igh MEE]

Translation: **I am**

Uses in John's Gospel: **9**

Uses in John's writings: **9**

Uses in the NT: **11**

Key passages: **John 4:26;
8:58; 18:5**

The words *ego eimi* occur numerous times in the NT, but in John's Gospel they have a special meaning with two related connotations. First, *I am* often refers to Jesus' claim to be the Messiah. This is clear in John 4 where the woman at the well referred to the coming Messiah (v. 25) and Jesus responded, "I am He [*ego eimi*]." This meaning of *ego eimi* also occurs in Jesus' words to the disciples, "I'm telling you now before it [Judas's betrayal] happens, so that when it does happen you will believe that I am He [*ego eimi*]" (13:19). Jesus' foreknowledge of Judas's betrayal provided evidence for the other disciples that He was indeed the Messiah. Second, *I am* often refers to Jesus' claim to deity and reflects the burning bush episode when God revealed Himself to Moses as "I am" (Ex 3:14). This meaning of *I am* occurs at Jesus' walking on the water (6:20; "It is I [*ego eimi*]"; see Mk 6:50; Lk 21:8), in a conversation with the Jewish leaders when Jesus stated that He existed prior to Abraham (8:58; "Before Abraham was, I am [*ego eimi*]"), and at Jesus' arrest when the soldiers attempting to find Him fell back to the ground on hearing Jesus say the words "I am He [*ego eimi*]" (18:5).

25 Righteous Father! The world has not known You.
However, I have known You,
and these have known that You sent Me.
26 I made Your name known to them and will make it known,
so that the love with which You have loved Me may be in them,
and that I may be in them."

JESUS BETRAYED

18 After Jesus had said these things, He went out with His disciples across the Kidron ravine,[a] where there was a garden into which He and His disciples entered. 2 Judas, who betrayed Him, also knew the place, because Jesus often met there with His disciples. 3 So Judas took a detachment of soldiers and some temple police from the chief priests and the Pharisees and came there with lanterns, torches, and weapons.

4 Then Jesus, knowing everything that was about to happen to Him, went out and said to them, "Who is it you're looking for?"

5 "Jesus the Nazarene," they answered.

"I am He,"[b] Jesus told them.

Judas, who betrayed Him, was also standing with them. 6 When He told them, "I am He," they stepped back and fell to the ground.

7 Then He asked them again, "Who is it you're looking for?"

"Jesus the Nazarene," they said.

8 "I told you I am He," Jesus replied. "So if you're looking for Me, let these men go." 9 This was to fulfill the words which He had said: "I have not lost one of those You have given Me."

10 Then Simon Peter, who had a sword, drew it, struck the high priest's slave, and cut off his right ear. (The slave's name was Malchus.)

11 At that, Jesus said to Peter, "Sheathe your sword! Should I not drink the cup that the Father has given Me?"

---

[a]18:1 Or *Kidron valley,* which was east of the temple complex in Jerusalem

[b]18:5, 8 Lit *I am* (see note at 8:58; Ex 3:13–14)

JESUS ARRESTED
AND TAKEN TO ANNAS

¹² Then the detachment of soldiers, the captain, and the Jewish temple police arrested Jesus and tied Him up. ¹³ First they led Him to Annas, for he was the father-in-law of Caiaphas, who was high priest that year. ¹⁴ Caiaphas was the one who had advised the Jews that it was advantageous that one man should die for the people.[a]

PETER DENIES JESUS

¹⁵ Meanwhile Simon Peter was following Jesus, as was another disciple. That disciple was an acquaintance of the high priest; so he went with Jesus into the high priest's courtyard. ¹⁶ But Peter remained standing outside by the door. So the other disciple, the one known to the high priest, went out and spoke to the girl who kept the door, and brought Peter in.

¹⁷ Then the slave-girl who kept the door said to Peter, "You aren't one of this man's disciples too, are you?"

"I am not!" he said. ¹⁸ Now the slaves and the temple police had made a charcoal fire, because it was cold. They were standing there warming themselves, and Peter was standing with them and warming himself.

JESUS BEFORE ANNAS

¹⁹ The high priest questioned Jesus about His disciples and about His teaching.

²⁰ "I have spoken openly to the world," Jesus answered him. "I have always taught in the synagogue and in the temple complex, where all the Jews congregate, and I haven't spoken anything in secret. ²¹ Why do you question Me? Question those who heard what I told them. Look, they know what I said."

²² When He had said these things, one of the temple police standing by slapped Jesus, saying, "Is this the way you answer the high priest?"

²³ "If I have spoken wrongly," Jesus answered him, "give evidence[b] about the wrong; but if rightly, why do you hit Me?"

²⁴ Then Annas sent Him bound to Caiaphas the high priest.

**Obedience Is
Worth Any Cost**

Although obedience is costly, it is always worth the cost. In fact, whenever you are tempted to consider the cost too high, you need to consider what it will cost you not to do the will of God. The cost is even greater.

At that, Jesus said to Peter, "Sheathe your sword! Should I not drink the cup that the Father has given Me?"

—John 18:11

---

[a]**18:14** 11:50   [b]**18:23** Or *testify*

PETER DENIES JESUS
TWICE MORE

[25] Now Simon Peter was standing and warming himself. They said to him, "You aren't one of His disciples too, are you?"

He denied it and said, "I am not!"

[26] One of the high priest's slaves, a relative of the man whose ear Peter had cut off, said, "Didn't I see you with Him in the garden?"

[27] Peter then denied it again. Immediately a rooster crowed.

JESUS BEFORE PILATE

[28] Then they took Jesus from Caiaphas to the governor's headquarters.[a] It was early morning. They did not enter the headquarters themselves; otherwise they would be defiled and unable to eat the Passover.

[29] Then Pilate[b] came out to them and said, "What charge do you bring against this man?"

[30] They answered him, "If this man weren't a criminal,[c] we wouldn't have handed Him over to you."

[31] So Pilate told them, "Take Him yourselves and judge Him according to your law."

"It's not legal[d] for us to put anyone to death," the Jews declared. [32] They said this so that Jesus' words might be fulfilled signifying what sort of death He was going to die.

[33] Then Pilate went back into the headquarters,[e] summoned Jesus, and said to Him, "Are You the King of the Jews?"

[34] Jesus answered, "Are you asking this on your own, or have others told you about Me?"

[35] "I'm not a Jew, am I?" Pilate replied. "Your own nation and the chief priests handed You over to me. What have You done?"

[36] "My kingdom is not of this world," said Jesus. "If My kingdom were of this world, My servants[f] would

---

Submit Yourself Freely to His Correction

Disobedience is never taken lightly by God. At times He lets you proceed in your disobedience, but He will never let you go too far without discipline to bring you back.

One of the high priest's slaves, a relative of the man whose ear Peter had cut off, said, "Didn't I see you with Him in the garden?" Peter then denied it again. Immediately a rooster crowed.

—John 18:26–27

---

[a]**18:28** I.e. the *praetorium,* the home of the governor of a Roman province

[b]**18:29** Pontius Pilate was appointed by Caesar Tiberius as the fifth governor of the province of Judea in A.D. 26. His jurisdiction included Samaria to the north, Gaza and the Dead Sea area to the south. He remained at this post until A.D. 36.

[c]**18:30** Lit *an evil doer*

[d]**18:31** I.e. according to Roman law

[e]**18:33** I.e. the *praetorium*

[f]**18:36** Or *attendants, helpers*

fight, so that I wouldn't be handed over to the Jews. As it is, My kingdom does not have its origin here."[a]

[37] "You are a king then?" Pilate asked.

"You say that I'm a king," Jesus replied. "I was born for this, and I have come into the world for this: to testify to the truth. Everyone who is of the truth listens to My voice."

[38] "What is truth?" said Pilate.

JESUS OR BARABBAS

After he had said this, he went out to the Jews again and told them, "I find no grounds for charging Him. [39] You have a custom that I release one prisoner[b] to you at the Passover. So, do you want me to release to you the King of the Jews?"

[40] They shouted back, "Not this man, but Barabbas!" Now Barabbas was a revolutionary.[c]

JESUS FLOGGED AND MOCKED

19 Then Pilate took Jesus and had Him flogged. [2] The soldiers also twisted a crown out of thorns, put it on His head, and threw a purple robe around Him. [3] And they repeatedly came up to Him and said, "Hail, king of the Jews!" and were slapping His face.

[4] Pilate went outside again and said to them, "Look, I'm bringing Him outside to you to let you know I find no grounds for charging Him."

PILATE SENTENCES
JESUS TO DEATH

[5] Then Jesus came out wearing the crown of thorns and the purple robe. Pilate said[d] to them, "Here is the man!"

[6] When the chief priests and the temple police saw Him, they shouted, "Crucify! Crucify!"

Pilate responded, "Take Him and crucify Him yourselves, for I find no grounds for charging Him."

[7] "We have a law," the Jews replied to him, "and

He Will Show You What He Wants You to Do

Truth is not discovered; it is revealed. Only God can tell you what He is doing or is wanting to do through your life. You will not be able to figure that out on your own.

"I have come into the world for this: to testify to the truth. Everyone who is of the truth listens to my voice."

—John 18:37b

---

[a]18:36 Lit *My kingdom is not from here*
[b]18:39 *prisoner* added for clarity
[c]18:40 Or *robber;* see 10:1,8 for the same Gk word used here
[d]19:5 Lit *He said*

according to that law He must die, because He made Himself[a] the Son of God."[b]

[8] When Pilate heard this statement, he was more afraid than ever. [9] He went back into the headquarters[c] and asked Jesus, "Where are You from?" But Jesus did not give him an answer. [10] So Pilate said to Him, "You're not talking to me? Don't You know that I have the authority to release You and the authority to crucify You?"

[11] "You would have no authority over Me at all," Jesus answered him, "if it hadn't been given you from above. This is why the one who handed Me over to you has the greater sin."[d]

[12] From that moment Pilate made every effort[e] to release Him. But the Jews shouted, "If you release this man, you are not Caesar's friend. Anyone who makes himself a king opposes Caesar!"

[13] When Pilate heard these words, he brought Jesus outside. He sat down on the judge's bench in a place called the Stone Pavement (but in Hebrew[f] Gabbatha). [14] It was the preparation day for the Passover, and it was about six in the morning.[g] Then he told the Jews, "Here is your king!"

[15] But they shouted, "Take Him away! Take Him away! Crucify Him!"

Pilate said to them, "Should I crucify your king?"

"We have no king but Caesar!" the chief priests answered.

[16] So then, because of them, he handed Him over to be crucified.

THE CRUCIFIXION

Therefore they took Jesus away. [17] Carrying His own cross, He went out to what is called Skull Place, which in Hebrew[h] is called Golgotha. [18] There they crucified Him and two others with Him, one on either side, with Jesus in the middle. [19] Pilate also had a sign lettered and put on the cross. The inscription was:

Obedience Is Always a Right-Now Event

The moment God speaks to you is the very moment God wants you to respond.

He said to His mother, "Woman, here is your son." Then He said to the disciple, "Here is your mother." And from that hour the disciple took her into his home.

—John 19:26b-27

---

[a]**19:7** I.e. He claimed to be
[b]**19:7** 5:18; 19:12
[c]**19:9** I.e. the *praetorium*
[d]**19:11** See note at 9:41
[e]**19:12** Lit *Pilate was trying*

[f]**19:13** I.e., Aramaic
[g]**19:14** Lit *the sixth hour;* or *about noon;* see note at 1:39
[h]**19:17, 20** I.e., Aramaic

JESUS THE NAZARENE
THE KING OF THE JEWS

[20] Many of the Jews read this sign, because the place where Jesus was crucified was near the city, and it was written in Hebrew,[a] Latin, and Greek. [21] So the chief priests of the Jews said to Pilate, "Don't write, 'The King of the Jews,' but that he said, 'I am the King of the Jews.'"

[22] Pilate replied, "What I have written, I have written."

[23] When the soldiers crucified Jesus, they took His clothes and divided them into four parts, a part for each soldier. They also took the tunic, which was seamless, woven in one piece from the top. [24] So they said to one another, "Let's not tear it, but toss for it, to see who gets it." They did this[b] to fulfill the Scripture which says: **"They divided My clothes among themselves, and for My clothing they cast lots."**[c] And this is what the soldiers did.

JESUS' PROVISION
FOR HIS MOTHER

[25] Standing by the cross of Jesus were His mother, His mother's sister, Mary the wife of Clopas, and Mary Magdalene.[d] [26] When Jesus saw His mother and the disciple He loved standing there, He said to His mother, "Woman, here is your son." [27] Then He said to the disciple, "Here is your mother." And from that hour the disciple took her into his home.

THE FINISHED WORK OF JESUS

[28] After this, when Jesus knew that everything was now accomplished, that the Scripture might be fulfilled, He said,[e] "I'm thirsty!" [29] A vessel full of sour wine was sitting there; so they fixed a sponge full of sour wine on hyssop[f] and held it up to His mouth.

---

[a]**19:17, 20** I.e. Aramaic
[b]**19:24** *They did this* supplied for clarity
[c]**19:24** Ps 22:18
[d]**19:25** Or *Mary of Magdala;* Magdala apparently was a town on the western shore of the Sea of Galilee and north of Tiberias.
[e]**19:28** Ps 69:21; see Jn 13:18; 17:12; 19:24
[f]**19:29** Or *with hyssop*

WORD STUDY

Greek word: **teleo** [tehl EH oh]
Translation: **finish**
Uses in John's Gospel: **2**
Uses in John's writings: **10**
Uses in the NT: **28**
Key passage: **John 19:28–30**

Just before His death on the cross, Jesus uttered a single word of victory: *tetelestai* [teh TEHL ehs tigh], "It is finished!" (Jn 19:30). The verb *teleo* is related to several other Greek words that refer to something being finished, accomplished, completed, or coming to an end. (The same verb is translated "accomplished" in v. 28.) The perfect tense of the Greek verb Jesus used indicates that He understood His death at this point in time to have abiding or lasting results. Jesus' death on the cross on our behalf was His purpose for coming into the world. It is not surprising that Revelation uses the term eight times, more than any other NT book, to describe various events related to Jesus' second coming (10:7; 11:7; 15:1,8; 17:17; 20:3,5,7).

³⁰ When Jesus had received the sour wine, He said, "It is finished!" Then bowing His head, He yielded up His spirit.

JESUS' SIDE PIERCED

³¹ Since it was the Preparation Day,ᵃ the Jews did not want the bodies to remain on the cross on the Sabbath (for that Sabbath was a specialᵇ day). They requested that Pilate have the men's legs broken and that their bodiesᶜ be taken away. ³² So the soldiers came and broke the legs of the first man and of the other one who had been crucified with Him. ³³ When they came to Jesus, they did not break His legs since they saw that He was already dead. ³⁴ But one of the soldiers pierced His side with a spear, and at once blood and water came out. ³⁵ He who saw this has testifiedᵈ so that you also may believe. His testimony is true, and he knows he is telling the truth.ᵉ ³⁶ For these things happened so that the Scripture may be fulfilled:ᶠ **"Not one of His bones will be broken."**ᵍ ³⁷ Also, another Scripture says: **"They will look at the One they pierced."**ʰ

JESUS' BURIAL

³⁸ After this, Joseph of Arimathea, who was a disciple of Jesus—but secretly because of his fear of the Jews—asked Pilate that he might remove the body of Jesus. Pilate gave him permission, so he came and took His body away. ³⁹ Nicodemus (who had previously come to Him at night) also came, bringing a mixture of about seventy-five poundsⁱ of myrrh and aloes. ⁴⁰ Then they took Jesus' body and wrapped it in linen cloths with the aromatic spices, according to the burial custom of the Jews. ⁴¹ There was a garden in the place where He was crucified. And in the garden was a new tomb in which no one had yet been placed. ⁴² So because of the Jewish Preparation Day, since the tomb was nearby, they placed Jesus there.

Watch the Way Jesus Did It

When I want to learn how to know and do the will of God, I always look to Jesus. I can find no better model than Him.

When Jesus had received the sour wine, He said, "It is finished!" Then bowing His head, He yielded up His spirit.

—John 19:30

ᵃ**19:31** 19:14
ᵇ**19:31** Lit *great*
ᶜ**19:31** *their bodies* added for clarity
ᵈ**19:35** 1:14,34
ᵉ**19:35** 21:24

ᶠ**19:36** 13:18; 17:12; 19:24
ᵍ**19:36** Ex 12:46; Num 9:12; Ps 34:20
ʰ**19:37** Zch 12:10
ⁱ **19:39** Lit *a hundred litrai* (a Roman *litrai* = twelve ounces)

THE EMPTY TOMB

20 On the first day of the week Mary Magdalene[a] came to the tomb early, while it was still dark. She saw that the stone had been removed[b] from the tomb. [2] So she ran to Simon Peter and to the other disciple, whom Jesus loved, and said to them, "They have taken the Lord out of the tomb, and we don't know where they have put Him!"

[3] At that, Peter and the other disciple went out, heading for the tomb. [4] The two were running together, but the other disciple outran Peter and got to the tomb first. [5] Stooping down, he saw the linen cloths lying there, yet he did not go in. [6] Then, following him, Simon Peter came also. He entered the tomb and saw the linen cloths lying there. [7] The wrapping which had been on His head was not lying with the linen cloths but folded up in a separate place by itself. [8] The other disciple, who had reached the tomb first, then entered the tomb, saw, and believed. [9] For they still did not understand the Scripture that He must rise from the dead. [10] Then the disciples went home again.

MARY MAGDALENE SEES THE RISEN LORD

[11] But Mary stood outside facing the tomb, crying. As she was crying, she stooped to look into the tomb. [12] She saw two angels in white sitting there, one at the head and one at the feet, where Jesus' body had been lying. [13] They said to her, "Woman,[c] why are you crying?"

"Because they've taken away my Lord," she told them, "and I don't know where they've put Him." [14] Having said this, she turned around and saw Jesus standing there, though she did not know it was Jesus.

[15] "Woman," Jesus said to her, "why are you crying? Who is it you are looking for?"

Supposing He was the gardener, she replied, "Sir, if you've removed Him, tell me where you've put Him, and I will take Him away."

[16] "Mary!" Jesus said.

Seek the Advice of Trustworthy Believers

Trust God to provide you counsel through other believers. Turn to them for counsel on major decisions. Listen attentively to anything the church has to say to you. Then let God confirm what His message is for you.

He who saw this has testified so that you also may believe. His testimony is true, and he knows he is telling the truth.

—John 19:35

---

[a]**20:1** See note at 19:25
[b]**20:1** Lit *She saw the stone removed*

[c]**20:13** See note at 2:4

WORD STUDY

Greek word: **pempo** [PEHM poh]
Translation: **send**
Uses in John's Gospel: **32**
Uses in John's writings: **37**
Uses in the NT: **79**
Key passages: **John 4:34; 20:21**

The Greek verb *pempo* is an old and common term meaning *to send*, reaching all the way back to the writings of Homer (eighth century B.C.). In John's Gospel, however, *pempo* emphasizes that someone is being sent by another of higher rank to perform a special task. Those who questioned John the Baptist had been sent (1:22) by the Pharisees (see v. 24), but John explained that he had been sent by God (v. 33). The Father will send the Holy Spirit (14:26), and so will Jesus (15:26; 16:7). On two occasions Jesus stated that He sends His disciples (13:20; 20:21). The dominant function of *pempo* is found in Jesus' use of the term to explain that the Father had sent Him. This aspect of *pempo* occurs twenty-three times in John's Gospel and has two connotations: first, to remind us of Jesus' divine origin, that He came from heaven where He had been with the Father (5:23; 6:38-39; 7:33; 8:16; 16:5); second, to emphasize that the Father gave Him a special task that only He could accomplish, the task of redemption (4:34; 6:44; 7:16,28). In the latter case, *pempo* takes on the meaning *commission* or *appoint*.

Turning around, she said to Him in Hebrew,[a] *"Rabbouni!"*[b]—which means "Teacher."

[17] "Don't cling to Me," Jesus told her, "for I have not yet ascended to the Father. But go to My brothers and tell them that I am ascending to My Father and your Father—to My God and your God."

[18] Mary Magdalene[c] went and announced to the disciples, "I have seen the Lord!" And she told them what[d] He had said to her.

THE DISCIPLES COMMISSIONED

[19] In the evening of that first day of the week, the disciples were gathered together[e] with the doors locked because of their fear of the Jews. Then Jesus came, stood among them, and said to them, "Peace to you!"[f]

[20] Having said this, He showed them His hands and His side. So the disciples rejoiced when they saw the Lord.

[21] Jesus said to them again, "Peace to you! Just as the Father has sent Me, I also send you."[g] [22] After saying this, He breathed on them and said,[h] "Receive the Holy Spirit. [23] If you forgive the sins of any, they are forgiven them; if you retain the sins of[i] any, they are retained."

THOMAS SEES AND BELIEVES

[24] But one of the twelve, Thomas (called "Twin"), was not with them when Jesus came. [25] So the other disciples kept telling him, "We have seen the Lord!"

But he said to them, "If I don't see the mark of the nails in His hands, put my finger into the mark of the nails, and put my hand into His side, I will never believe!"

[26] After eight days His disciples were indoors again, and Thomas was with them. Even though the doors were locked, Jesus came and stood among them. He said, "Peace to you!"

[27] Then He said to Thomas, "Put your finger here and

---

[a]**20:16** I.e. Aramaic
[b]**20:16** See note at 1:38; *Rabbouni* is used in Mark 10:51 also.
[c]**20:18** See note at 19:25
[d]**20:18** Lit *these things*
[e]**20:19** *gathered together* added for clarity

[f]**20:19** 14:27; 16:33
[g]**20:21** 13:20; 17:18
[h]**20:22** Lit *He breathed and said to them*
[i]**20:23** *the sins of* supplied for clarity

observe My hands. Reach out your hand and put it into My side. Don't be an unbeliever but a believer."

28 Thomas responded to Him, "My Lord and My God!"

29 Jesus said, "Because you have seen Me, you have believed.[a] Blessed are those who believe without seeing."

THE PURPOSE OF THIS GOSPEL

30 Jesus performed many other signs in the presence of His disciples which are not written in this book.
31 But these are written so that you may believe Jesus is the Messiah,[b] the Son of God,[c] and that by believing you may have life in His name.

JESUS' THIRD APPEARANCE TO THE DISCIPLES

21 After this, Jesus revealed Himself again to His disciples by the Sea of Tiberias.[d] He revealed Himself in this way:

2 Simon Peter, Thomas (called "Twin"), Nathanael from Cana of Galilee, Zebedee's sons, and two others of His disciples were together.

3 "I'm going fishing," Simon Peter said to them.

"We're coming with you," they told him. They went out and got into the boat; but that night they caught nothing.

4 When daybreak came, Jesus stood[e] on the shore. However, the disciples did not know that it was Jesus.[f]

5 "Men,"[g] Jesus called to them, "you don't have any fish, do you?"

"No," they answered.

6 "Cast the net on the right side of the boat," He told them, "and you'll find some." So they did,[h] and they were unable to haul it in because of the large number of fish. 7 Therefore the disciple whom Jesus loved said to Peter, "It's the Lord!"

When Simon Peter heard that it was the Lord, he tied his outer garment around him[i] (for he was stripped) and

God's Will Is Always Right, Though Not Always Reasonable

When you do what He tells you, no matter how unsensible it may seem, God accomplishes what He purposed through you. Not only do you experience God's power and presence, but so do those who observe what you are doing.

"Men," Jesus called to them, "you don't have any fish, do you?" "No," they answered. "Cast the net on the right side of the boat," He told them, "and you'll find some." So they did, and they were unable to haul it in because of the large number of fish.

—John 21:5–6

---

[a]20:29 Or *have you believed?*
[b]20:31 Or *the Christ*
[c]20:31 Or *that the Messiah, the Son of God, is Jesus*
[d]21:1 I.e. the Sea of Galilee; *Sea of Tiberias* is used only in John (see 6:1,23)
[e]21:4 20:14,19,26
[f]21:4 20:14
[g]21:5 Lit *children*
[h]21:6 Lit *they cast*
[i]21:7 Lit *he girded his garment*

WORD STUDY

Greek word: **phileo** [fihl EH oh]
Translation: **love**
Uses in John's Gospel: **13**
Uses in John's writings: **15**
Uses in the NT: **25**
Key passage: **John 21:15-17**

Although *agapao* (verb) and *agape* (noun) are normally considered the Greek words for divine love, the verb *phileo* can be used in the same way. The *phileo* word family has thirty-three terms used in the NT, including *philos (friend), philadelphia (Philadelphia* or *brotherly love),* and *philema (kiss).* The verb *phileo* can refer to the wrong kind of love (Mt 6:5; 10:37; 23:6 Lk 20:46; Jn 12:25; 15:19; Rev 22:15), as can *agapao* (Lk 11:43; Jn 3:19; 12:43; 2 Tim 4:10; 2 Pet 2:15; 1 Jn 2:15). But *phileo* is also used to describe the Father's love for the Son (Jn 5:20), the Father's love for believers (Jn 16:27), Jesus' love for believers (Jn 11:3; 20:2; Rev 3:19), and believers' love for the Lord (1 Cor 16:22) and for each other (Titus 3:15). Both *agapao* (Jn 13:23; 19:26; 21:7,20) and *phileo* (Jn 20:2) are used to describe "the disciple Jesus loved," and the meaning is the same. Thus, it is a mistake to make a sharp distinction in John 21:15–17 between *agapao* (Jesus' term in vv. 15,16) and *phileo* (Jesus' term in v. 17 and all three times by Peter). This is especially true since three other pairs of synonyms occur in this passage with no significant difference in meaning *(know,* v. 15/*know,* v. 17; *feed/shepherd; lambs/sheep).* In this context, both *agapao* and *phileo* refer to love in its purest form, so Peter's threefold confession of his love for Jesus, which corresponds to his earlier threefold denial of Him, should not be understood as a secondary form of love.

plunged into the sea. [8] But since they were not far from land (about a hundred yards away[a]), the other disciples came in the boat, dragging the net full of fish. [9] When they got out on land, they saw a charcoal fire there, with fish lying on it, and bread.

[10] "Bring some of the fish you've just caught," Jesus told them. [11] So Simon Peter got up and hauled the net ashore, full of large fish—153 of them. Even though there were so many, the net was not torn.

[12] "Come and have breakfast," Jesus told them. None of the disciples dared ask Him, "Who are You?" because they knew it was the Lord. [13] Jesus came, took the bread, and gave it to them. He did the same with the fish.

[14] This was now the third time[b] Jesus appeared[c] to the disciples after He was raised from the dead.

JESUS' THREEFOLD RESTORATION OF PETER

[15] When they had eaten breakfast, Jesus asked Simon Peter, "Simon, son of John,[1] do you love[d] me more than these?"

"Yes, Lord," he said to Him, "You know that I love You."

"Feed My lambs," He told him.

[16] A second time He asked him, "Simon, son of John, do you love Me?"

"Yes, Lord," he said to Him, "You know that I love You."

"Shepherd My sheep," He told him.

[17] He asked him the third time, "Simon, son of John, do you love Me?"

Peter was grieved that He asked him the third time, "Do you love Me?" He said, "Lord, You know everything! You know that I love You."

"Feed My sheep," Jesus said. [18] "I assure you:[e] When

[1]**21:15-17** Other mss read *Jonah;* see note at 1:42; Mt 16:17

[a]**21:8** Lit *two hundred cubits*
[b]**21:14** The other two are in 20:19–29.
[c]**21:14** Lit *was revealed* (see v. 1)
[d]**21:15-17** Two synonyms are translated *love* in this conversation: *agapao,* the first two times by Jesus

(vv. 15,16); and *phileo,* the last time by Jesus (v. 17) and all three times by Peter (vv. 15,16,17). Peter's threefold confession of love for Jesus corresponds to his earlier threefold denial of Jesus (18:15–18, 25–27).
[e]**21:18** See note at 1:51

you were young, you would tie your belt and walk wherever you wanted. But when you grow old, you will stretch out your hands and someone else will tie you and carry you where you don't want to go." [19] He said this to signify by what kind of death he would glorify God.[a] After saying this, He told him, "Follow Me!"[b]

CORRECTING A FALSE REPORT

[20] So Peter turned around and saw the disciple Jesus loved following them. That disciple[c] was the one who had leaned back against Jesus at the supper and asked, "Lord, who is the one that's going to betray You?" [21] When Peter saw him, he said to Jesus, "Lord—what about him?"

[22] "If I want him to remain until I come," Jesus answered, "what is that to you? As for you, follow Me."

[23] So this report[d] spread to the brothers[e] that this disciple would not die. Yet Jesus did not tell him that he would not die, but, "If I want him to remain until I come, what is that to you?"

EPILOGUE

[24] This is the disciple who testifies to these things and who wrote them down. We know that his testimony is true.

[25] And there are also many other things that Jesus did, which, if they were written one by one, I suppose not even the world itself could contain the books[f] that would be written.

Your Part in God's Will Is Simply to Follow It

The servant does not tell the Master what kind of assignments he needs. The servant waits on his Master for the assignment.

When Peter saw him, he said to Jesus, "Lord—what about him?" "If I want him to remain until I come," Jesus answered, "what is that to you? As for you, follow Me."

—John 21:21–22

---

[a]**21:19** Jesus predicts that Peter would be martyred. Church tradition says that Peter was crucified upside down.
[b]**21:19** 1:43; 8:12; 10:27

[c]**21:20** *That disciple* added for clarity
[d]**21:23** Lit *this word*
[e]**21:23** The word *brothers* refers to the whole Christian community.
[f]**21:25** Lit *scrolls*

Code for Pronunciation[1]
of Greek words in the Word Studies

CODE	EXAMPLE	CODE	EXAMPLE
a	HAT	oo	LOOK
ah	far, FAHR	oo	boot, BOOT
aw	call, KAWL		
ay	name, NAYM	ow	cow, KOW
b	BAD		out, OWT
ch	CHEW	oy	boil, BOYL
d	DAD	p	PAT
e, eh	met, MEHT	r	RAN
ee	sea, SEE	s	star, STAHR
	ski, SKEE		tsetse, SET see
ew	truth, TREWTH	sh	show, SHOH
f	FOOT		action, AK shuhn
	enough, ee NUHF		mission, MIH shuhn
g	GET		vicious, VIH shuhss
h	HIM	t	tie, TIGH
hw	whether, HWEH thuhr		Thomas, TAH muhss
i, ih	city, SIH tih	th	thin, THIHN, THIN
igh	sign, SIGHN	th	there, THEHR
	eye, IGH	tw	TWIN
igh	lite, LIGHT	u,uh	tub, TUHB
ih	pin, PIHN, PIN		Joshua JAHSH yew uh
j	jack, JAK		term TUHRM
	germ JUHRM	v	veil, VAYL
k	KISS		of, AHV
	cow, KOW	w	WAY
ks	ox, AHKS		
kw	quail, KWAYL	wh	(whether) see hw
l	live, LIHV, LIGHV	y	year, YEER
m	more, MOHR	z	xerox, ZIHR ahks
n	note, NOHT		ZEE rahks
ng	ring, RING		his, HIHZ, HIZ
oh	go, GOH		zebra, ZEE bruh
	row, ROH (a boat)	zh	version, VUHR zhuhn

[1]This "Code for Pronunciation" is taken from the book by W. Murray Severance, *That's Easy for You to Say: Your Quick Guide to Pronouncing Bible Names* (Nashville: Broadman & Holman Publishers, 1997). Used by permission of the author.

Pray with Us
Pray for us

Clear communication of God's word is an awe-inspiring responsibility that reaches its greatest heights when anyone attempts to accurately translate His written word from one language into another. The heartcry of every member of the Holman Christian Standard Bible™ translation team is to render God's word accurately, faithfully, and in a way that will declare His glory for generations to come. It is a calling beyond the scope of human wit and intelligence alone. The active hand of God Himself is needed to produce a faithful, precise rendering of His word. To that end, we invite you to join us in praying regularly for the Holman CSB™ translation work.

If you believe God would have you join us as a prayer partner, please complete the commitment below and send it or a photocopy to Holman Bibles. In appreciation of your response, we will update you regularly on our progress through the translation newsletter. It will not only tell you how the work is progressing but will also aid you in knowing how to pray for the process.

Please join us.

- -

Name _____

Address _____

Phone _____ E-mail _____

Church Affiliation _____

What best describes your role in your Church?   pastor ____ staff ____

Sunday School teacher ____ church officer ____ other: _____

My commitment: During the next year, I will pray for the translation work

daily _____ weekly _____ other: _____

Send your commitment to:

Holman Bibles Translation Prayer Team
MSN 164
127 Ninth Avenue North
Nashville, TN 37234

Or send an e-mail with the above information to:

www.broadmanholman@lifeway.com